Christians and the
New Creation

Christians and the New Creation

*Genesis Motifs
in the New Testament*

Paul Sevier Minear

Westminster John Knox Press
Louisville, Kentucky

To Beth, Deedee, and Fritz
for good reasons

Scripture quotations from the New Revised Standard Version of the Bible are copyright © 1989 by the Division of Christian Education of the National Council of the Churches of Christ in the U.S.A., and are used by permission.

Book and cover design by Drew Stevens

First edition

Published by Westminster John Knox Press
Louisville, Kentucky

This book is printed on acid-free paper that meets the American National Standards Institute Z39.48 standard. ∞

PRINTED IN THE UNITED STATES OF AMERICA
94 95 96 97 98 99 00 01 02 03 04   10 9 8 7 6 5 4 3 2 1

Library of Congress Cataloging-in-Publication Data

Minear, Paul Sevier, date.
    Christians and the new creation : Genesis motifs in the New
Testament / Paul Sevier Minear. — 1st ed.
        p.   cm.
    Includes bibliographical references and index.
    ISBN 0-664-25531-0
    1. Bible.   N.T.—Relation to Genesis.   2. Bible.   O.T.   Genesis—
Relation to the New Testament.   3. Bible   N.T.—Theology.
4. Bible.   O.T.   Genesis—Theology.   I. Title
BS2387.M56   1994
220.9'2—dc20   93-42167

Contents

Acknowledgments   vii

Prologue: Stages in the Study   ix

1. Peace on Earth: The Promise of the
   Covenant in Luke   1

2. Jesus and Satan: The Sealing of the
   Covenant in Luke   31

3. Adam and Christ: Death and Life in
   1 Corinthians 15   62

4. Works of God: The Two Families in
   John's Gospel   82

5. From One Covenant to Another:
   Metaphors of Transition   103

Selected Writings by Paul Sevier Minear,
   compiled by Richard H. Minear   131

Index   139

Acknowledgments

For comments on the manuscript at various stages, I thank Brevard S. Childs, Susan R. Garrett, Kendrick L. Norris, and Mary-Lynn Ogletree. For compilation of the bibliography I thank Richard H. Minear. For word processing skills I thank Robert Whitaker and Larry Minear. For improvements in style and substance and for constant encouragement I thank Gladys H. Minear.

Quotations from the Bible and the Apocrypha are drawn from the New Revised Standard Version, except where I have indicated the use of my own translation or paraphrase.

Prologue

Stages in the Study

You always find what you are looking for in the last place you look.

The length of a Bible study is always unpredictable. When a simple question yields an obvious answer, the study ends almost at once. If, however, the question does not prove to be so simple, the search for answers may lead on and on and on. So it has proved to be with the question with which this study began. The familiar story of the visit by angels to the Bethlehem shepherds prompted this question: Did the angelic promise of peace on earth have any connection with the original story of violence on earth, Cain's murder of his brother Abel? In that case of violence, the earth cried out to God with the blood of Abel. Thus I asked whether, in Luke's mind, the announcement of a final peace on earth canceled the primal curse of murder on earth. Quite unexpectedly, the search for answers came to require, step by step, the study of both volumes of Luke's writing and to lead beyond Luke to the rest of the New Testament.

A Bible study is also unpredictable in the confidence one can have in the results. A study may begin with a high degree of confidence in a first set of conclusions but may end quickly in almost complete disillusionment. Or it may begin with a high degree of skepticism and end with an equally high degree of confidence. So it has been with the exploration of possible connections between the Genesis traditions of God's curse on the first rebellious creatures and the Lukan saga of prophecies, visions, annunciations, the ministry of Jesus, and the mission of his messengers. Hypothetical possibilities with regard to the linkage between the primal covenant and the final covenant became increasingly probable as the study proceeded.

Finally, a Bible study is unpredictable in its potential importance. The current study is a case in point. At the outset, the importance was

limited to an understanding of a brief episode of some twelve verses
in a single Gospel, an episode not referred to later, either in that
Gospel or elsewhere in the New Testament. It had to do with a matter that seemed to be of concern only to professional exegetes: Was
Luke's imaginative portrait of the shepherds painted in a studio
where the painter was in any degree influenced by the Genesis pictures of the murder of the first shepherd? In the end, the story has
come, almost without any such expectation, to involve the early Christian understandings of the two creations, old and new—matters of
primal and final importance. That involvement has led, in turn, to
understandings of how individuals and churches conceived of their
own participation in the transition from the old age to the new. Thus
a study that began with questions about peace on earth has come to
require a fresh examination of how individuals come to share in the
new covenant in Christ's blood.

The study actually began much earlier than my interest in the
questions raised by the angels' message to the shepherds. It began
with a casual exploration of the influence that the Genesis curse on
Cain had on an esoteric text in the Apocalypse. When I started that
exploration I had no inkling that it would lead into so many nooks
and crannies of early Christian reflections on the gospel. Beginning
at that point, the study has moved forward in a zigzag fashion from
Genesis to the New Testament and back again and from one early
Christian author to another. Because the journey was not planned in
advance, reports on the landscape cannot be organized around a single theme and pigeonholed under such familiar captions as the life
of Jesus or basic Christian beliefs. So, to minimize confusion, I will
outline here in chronological order the major stages in my journey.

On retirement from my teaching post in Yale Divinity School, I accepted an appointment in Jerusalem as vice rector of the new Ecumenical Institute for Advanced Theological Research (commonly
called Tantur). Because I expected to devote myself full-time to the
direction of this promising venture, I abandoned any thought of carrying on further research of my own. I gave most of my books to the
library at the Institute to provide grist for other scholars. As often
happens, such plans "gang aft a-gley." The climate in Jerusalem declared war on my health; after two years it won the battle, and I left
the field of conflict.

Returning to the States, I took up residence at some distance from
previous university haunts. In my new habitat the local church supplanted the ecumenical, and lay involvements replaced the academic. I had no more daily visits to the university library or frequent

conversations with exegetes and theologians. I learned how quickly the cessation of academic routines makes one an alien in the former homeland. Until retirement, my two vocations had been closely aligned—ordination as a Christian minister and appointments to teach in theological seminaries. After retirement the first remained strong while the other tended to atrophy, even though on occasion I taught at various schools and wrote on various subjects.

During recent years a major share of energy has been devoted to the translation committee that prepared the New Revised Standard Version of the Bible (NRSV). With its publication in 1990 I anticipated a second retirement, with no obligation to teach or to write. As one way to celebrate this new respite from work, I decided to use my leisure time to read what some colleagues in the NRSV work had done. Since I had been engrossed in the New Testament, I decided to read in random fashion some books in the Old Testament and in the Apocrypha. I enjoyed the hours of reading in these books, for I found that my colleagues in the Old Testament had succeeded in using an imaginative freshness of idiom that gave new potencies to familiar texts. As a New Testament exegete I was fascinated to discover many intertextual linkages between the Testaments, passages in the Old that added unsuspected resonance to the texts in the New.

It was when I stumbled on one of those linkages that the luxury of this second retirement was disturbed and that, almost against my natural inclination, I began to reread, with a new set of questions, one New Testament passage after another. I had been enjoying the new translation of Genesis and had reached chapter 4 when I noticed a strange coincidence between the Genesis account of the earth's reaction to the murder of Abel and the account in Revelation of the earth's reaction to the murder of Christian martyrs. In Genesis, when the earth had opened its mouth to receive the blood of Abel, that blood had cried out to God, and God had cursed the murder "from the earth" (Gen. 4:10–12). When I read those verses, I recalled the passage in the Apocalypse that has long puzzled commentators. There, too, the earth had played a decisive role at a strategic time by opening its mouth to swallow an evil drink. But in this case the curse had been replaced by a blessing (Rev. 12:13–17). The "ancient serpent" (the same destructive power as in Genesis 3) had been pursuing the mother of the Messiah (pictured as the second Eve), a flood pouring from its mouth; but the earth had opened its mouth, swallowing the flood and saving the mother. The two texts were very different, but in both the earth had played a strategic symbolic role. I felt impelled to explore the possibility that the Genesis text provided a missing clue to meanings imbedded in the Apocalypse. As usual, when a veteran teacher embarks on such an exploration, the result was an essay, which in this instance was published in *Novum Testamentum*.[1]

Having succeeded in showing, at least to my own satisfaction, that the Genesis curse on the earth had been removed by a blessing on the earth, I began to wonder whether a similar role had been assigned to the earth in other books of the New Testament. My attention gravitated to a baffling episode in the Gospel of John in which Jesus is pictured, during the judgment scene on the adulteress, as writing on the earth not once but twice. What was the symbolic weight of the earth in that scene (John 8:2–11)? The Pharisees had brought to Jesus a woman seized in the act, asking him whether the penalty commanded by Moses should be inflicted. In reply, Jesus had spoken first to the judges and then to the woman; but in each case his spoken word had been preceded by his writing on the earth. Why did he do that? What did he write? How should one interpret his actions? On exploring the possible connections between Genesis and Gospel, I again found convincing evidence that the primeval curse on the earth provided a clue to Jesus' action. That curse was removed in Jesus' announcement of God's judgment on the human judges and of God's mercy on the condemned sinner.[2]

With two such instances of the removal of the primordial curse on the earth, I began to wonder whether a third instance might occur in the Lukan birth story, in which the angelic choir praised God for granting peace on earth to those whom he favored. Was this instance, too, a way of announcing a divine blessing that replaced a divine curse? In this case, the search for corroborating data became much more extensive. Against all expectation, it led me into an examination of the whole of Luke's two volumes, and it involved not only the Genesis curse on the earth but the entire series of curses in Genesis 3 and 4 and the entire picture of the sins of Eve, Adam, and Cain for which those curses were the continuing penalty. Indeed, the question soon emerged as to how Luke's understanding of the new creation in Christ had been shaped by the Genesis story of Creation and Fall. Studies of Luke-Acts disclosed increasing evidence that the Genesis saga had helped to inform not only the story of the shepherds but the story of Mary, the story of Jesus, and the story of the apostles (see chapters 1 and 2 below). Yet this evidence was so subtle and so submerged within the narrative theology of Luke that I found it helpful first to examine other major literary traditions, such as the Pauline and the Johannine, in which the influence of Genesis was more explicit. A survey of this influence I first included as a preface to the Lukan study, hoping that it would make more persuasive my reading of Luke's theology, but it soon became far too extensive to include in a study of Luke.

Now, to the next link in the chain of studies released by my casual reading of Genesis. When, as a possible preface to the Lukan study, I surveyed the Pauline tradition, I noticed afresh the concentration of echoes in 1 Corinthians 15. Not only was the importance of Adam dominant in Paul's understanding of sin and death, but also many more subdued echoes showed the pervasive influence of Genesis: the contrasts between the man from earth and the man from heaven; the work of the Creator in producing the flesh of earthly bodies (beasts, birds, fish, human beings) and the glory of heavenly bodies (sun, moon, stars); the contrasts between the primal goodness and the frustrations of futile labor; the struggle of Paul with the wild beasts; the dominion of humanity over the other creatures (given, forfeited, restored); the universal range of God's grace at the beginning and at the end.

Approaching this familiar chapter from this new angle, I was surprised at how many new implications seemed to leap from Paul's sentences. I could follow more easily the flow of his argument, which became more convincing when approached from this perspective, that is, from a world of thought in which the story in Genesis was not merely a story but served as a map of Paul's thought world. So, for my own sake, I began to jot down on paper the course of Paul's debate with his original readers, realizing that the course of my own debate with him followed similar lines. Turning back and forth from Genesis to Paul, I became amazed at the intertextual density of his thinking (see chapter 3 below). The prominence of this kind of thinking in 1 Corinthians 15 induced me to survey the entire New Testament, selecting metaphorical descriptions of the transitions made by Christians in moving from one covenant with God to a new bonding in Christ. In many instances the new bonds were initiated by a sharing in Christ's blood, and the descriptions of those bonds reverberated with strong echoes of the Genesis stories. Thus it was that I came to write the twelve thumbnail sketches that appear as chapter 5.

In those sketches I kept encountering leads to and into the Gospel of John, most often to the Prologue with its account of beginnings. The Prologue is clearly patterned to match the Genesis story, with its appeal to the primacy of God's word and its image of God begetting children through his word. I found that I could not terminate that investigation short of a study of the whole Gospel (see chapter 4 below). That study of John became the last link in a chain of explorations that began with a chance reading of Genesis 4, with its picture of the earth drinking the blood of the first victim of human hatred and violence. Following the trail of the blood of Abel, I was led to fresh appreciations of the covenant that was celebrated whenever early Christian communities drank the blood of the new covenant. To them that covenant became an assurance of peace on earth, where everything old had passed away, including the curses of Genesis 3.

How important are these echoes of Genesis in the New Testament? As a result of this study I have an increased respect for Jesus and his messengers, all of whom treated the traditions of Creation and Fall with utmost seriousness. Let me summarize four ways in which they manifested that seriousness.

First, they accepted the tradition of creation as essential for an understanding of the universality and inclusiveness of the good news. "Just as in Adam *all*, . . . so also in Christ *all*. . . ." The range of vision is unlimited, as is the inclusion of all creation. Only with this assurance could Paul assert that there is neither Jew nor Greek in Christ, neither male nor female, neither oppressor nor oppressed.

Second, the appeal to origins offered apostles the only way to fathom the abysmal depth and age-long power of evil: "Just as one man's trespass led to condemnation for all"—this idea enabled them to attest the greater depth and enduring power of God's grace—"so one man's act of righteousness leads to justification and life for all" (Rom. 5:18). The measure of slavery became the measure of liberation. The blood of Abel, the blood of Christ—each served, by contrast, as a way of measuring the other.

Third, the reflections on Genesis helped to focus attention on the primal designs of the Creator. When apostles wrote "in the beginning" or "from the foundation of the world," they were thinking not so much of *how* God created all things as of *why*, not so much of dates on a cosmic calendar as of God's continuing purposes. Those purposes determined the reality hidden in every situation, which affected the secret purposes of every creature. It was God's creating will that led God to subject all creation to futility "in hope that the creation itself will be set free from its bondage to decay" (Rom. 8:20–21). That same creating will led God to call those who loved him and to predestine them "to be conformed to the image of his Son" (Rom. 8:28–30). Every sibling of Jesus, along with the entire family of the "firstborn," received a vocation stamped "in the beginning." "You did not choose me but I chose you . . . to . . . ." (John 15:16).

Finally, it is clear that the apostles' visions of the future were shaped to match these communal memories of the past, Omega perspectives matching Alpha perspectives. A sample of Alpha thinking is: "The law of the Spirit of life [a faint echo of Genesis] in Christ Jesus has set you free from the law of sin and of death [a clear allusion to Genesis]" (Rom. 8:2). A sample of Omega thinking: "I am convinced that neither death, nor life, . . . nor things present, nor things to come . . . will be able to separate us from the love of God in Christ Jesus our Lord" (Rom. 8:38–39). Even more condensed is the formula in the Epistle to the Hebrews, bonding God's design for the future to his creative action at the beginning: The Son whom God appointed as heir of all things is the one through whom he created the ages (Heb. 1:2). A similar pattern of convictions led the prophet John to visualize in the new earth the very tree of life from which Adam had been banished (Rev. 22:2; Gen. 3:24).

Not long ago an American, Aaron Latham, was for the first time visiting a ranch in Kenya near the region where traces of the earliest human habitation have been found. His account of that visit included this puzzlement: "I felt at home here . . . really at home . . . and yet I had never been to Kenya before, never even been to Africa before. . . . I belonged to this place where I was an alien. I was a stranger, but not in a strange land, not at all."[3] Latham asked many people why this should be true, but he was not satisfied with the answers. Finally he talked with Richard Leakey, anthropologist son of the famous scientist who had worked in Kenyan excavations for many years. This scientist gave him an answer that clicked: "genetic memory—a memory, almost a familiarity; it is very primitive." Leakey was confident of this answer even though he admitted that he had no scientific basis for it.

Christians often point to comparable experiences when they read the story of creation in Genesis and sense its linkage to creative forces at work today. They express that sense when they sing "Morning has broken like the first morning" or "How brightly shines the morning star." When they read about the effect on God's creation of deception, lies, thorns, thistles, human violence, they recognize the same destructive forces at work in their own families and nations. A similar genetic spiritual memory is active when Christians read accounts of Jesus' death for their sins. "Were you there when they crucified my Lord?" "Amazing grace, how sweet the sound." Or in Advent season when the carol of Isaac Watts reminds them that "his blessings flow far as the curse is found." Or when they hear Paul's shout of victory: "Where, O Death, is your sting?" or join in singing John's Hallelujah

Chorus: "And he shall reign forever and ever." This genetic spiritual memory of the primal conflict between the Adamic and the Christic forces can reveal even to sophisticated moderns an imaginative transcript of the ultimate beginnings and endings of their own desires and decisions, whether as individuals or as members of the families of both Adams.

Notes

1. "Far as the Curse Is Found: The Point of Revelation 12:15–16," *Novum Testamentum* 33 (1991): 71–77.
2. "Writing on the Ground: The Puzzle in John 8:1–11," *Horizons in Biblical Theology* 13 (1991): 23–37.
3. *New York Times,* 10 Nov. 1991, Magazine section.

1
Peace on Earth

The Promise of the Covenant in Luke

God's appearance has now become the news of the day. . . .
The news of the day the beginning of eternity![1]

This essay in biblical theology is designed primarily for Christian ministers engaged in their vocation as interpreters of the Bible. It focuses attention on the kinds of thinking about God that one meets in the Bible. The essay examines patterns of thinking about God's work as creator, maker, founder, king, father—images with which early Christians conveyed their understanding of their own roots. Whenever they used the image of God as creator, they usually referred, whether explicitly or implicitly, to accounts in the opening chapters of Genesis. Accordingly, whenever the image of a new creation emerged, those same chapters served as a useful foil for their ideas; to them the new creation was both like and unlike the old.

The Genesis saga of creation moved almost immediately from the account of God's commands on seven successive days to the incitements to rebellion on the part of God's creatures, from the unconditional goodness of Genesis 1 and 2 to the eruption of tragic alienation in Genesis 3 and 4. Thus it is impossible to separate God's work as creator from the tragic appearance of abysmal evil. In their thinking about the new age, early Christians took with utmost seriousness the corrosive legacy of the sins of Eve, Adam, and Cain, along with the resulting curses leveled on them by their Creator.

But to mention these sins and curses is to lose many readers. Most ministers in American Protestant churches have been trained in seminaries that give little serious attention to the curses in Genesis 3 and 4. Teachers have often treated those curses as little more than examples of etiological legends with no enduring significance. Like many other such legends in primitive societies, they explain why things are as they are: Why snakes slither along the ground on their bellies. Why human beings try to kill snakes by bashing in their heads. Why the process of bearing children is so painful. Seldom do modern theologians interpret those curses as profound clues to God's way of dealing with the old age or as providing a rationale for God's creation of a new age. Nothing in American culture encourages us to trace the origin of massive, inherited evil to such origins.

It is not surprising, then, that whenever someone suggests the possibility of linking either damnation or salvation to these stories, a large cluster of allergies creates subtle but effective resistance. For one thing, we are uncomfortable with the important roles assigned to the serpent and with the identification of that serpent with Satan. For a generation we have disavowed belief in the devil as deceiver, in "original sin," in the inheritance of sin, and in the link between such an inheritance and death. The New Testament images of ransom and atonement have ceased to be cogent descriptions of radical changes in our condition as heirs of Adam and captives of Satan, sin, and death. The once-powerful language of blood—whether the blood of Abel, of the Passover lamb, of Jesus, or of the new covenant—has quietly slipped out of our vocabulary, though not out of the hymns we sing. We long ago jettisoned the traditional doctrines of election and predestination that drew their original force from victories in the age-long warfare between God and the devil. We fear that to take seriously the Genesis account of the Fall might entangle us again in the literalism of those who have turned "creationism" into the litmus test of Christian faith. "No, thank you," we say. "We have had enough of that kind of return to the roots."

I urge readers to continue with me in spite of such real allergies. The search for origins is highly characteristic of our time; ministers, of all people, should be aware of its diverse forms and latent power. For example, in designing and sending into orbit the Hubble telescope, astrophysicists have been confident of learning important things about the beginnings of this vast universe. Biochemists have been succeeding in isolating and picturing the genes that form the cells of the human body so that they might explain the dysfunctioning of those cells, developing their own myths of biological creation and fall. Psychiatrists persevere in a ministry of healing by way of pursuing archetypal fantasies and phobias to their hidden roots so that they may open the way for a return to psychic health. Many ethnic groups evoke revolutionary power by identifying current oppressive tyrannies with the "Fall" in order that they may recover through political change their mythical Edens. In many disciplines of mind and body it is necessary to begin again with the ABCs, or in a more recent idiom, with Square One; and in each of those disciplines resistance to a return is provided by apparently immovable obstacles. Those who want most desperately to return home find that they can't go home again. The goodness of the beginning and the evil of alienation from it are twin recognitions, born in the same moment. To deny either would be an act of self-deception, dishonesty, and defeat. When one draws up a transcript of current human experience in any major human endeavor, one finds an analogue to the Genesis accounts of Creation and Fall—and to the messianic hope of a new beginning.

Christians, however, have much deeper reasons for their perennial interest in Genesis. We have our own roots to discover and rediscover. Who are we, if not children of a heavenly parent, brothers and sisters of God's Son, members of a distinctive family, and therefore members of one another? As the apostle insisted: "If anyone is in Christ, there is a new creation" (2 Cor. 5:17). But what does that mean? Some of the meanings are imbedded in the familiar benediction of 2 Cor. 13:13.

"The grace of the Lord Jesus Christ"—that grace is as primal as it is contemporary. It is an amazing gift that defines us as those who have migrated from one age to another, as blind persons who now can see. The power of such grace is measured by the depth of the dereliction it overcomes, that is, God's curse.

"The love of God"—that love has made us his children. Such love originated long before any moment in an individual's lifetime; it must be traced back at least as far as the crucifixion of Jesus, where the collision between love and hatred marked the invasive power of God's new creation.

"The communion of the Holy Spirit"—that communion is the root-life of a community that can be understood only in terms of a specific origin as described in the scriptures. In them, birth through the Spirit is distinguished from natural birth, just as the present communion is distinguished from all previous solidarities. By these phrases the benediction silently testifies to both personal and communal transition from one age to another. The other benedictions in the New Testament also point to the reality and the radicality of such a migration.

What was true of early Christian benedictions was also true of their salutations. Their common perspectives were encapsulated in Paul's greeting to his readers in Galatia; together they celebrated their emancipation from the age of rebellion to the age ruled by grace and peace. "Grace to you and peace from God our Father and the Lord Jesus Christ, who gave himself for our sins to set us free from the present evil age, according to the will of our God and Father, to whom be the glory forever and ever. Amen" (Gal. 1:3–5). One can have little doubt that Paul here traced the beginning of the evil age to the first Adam and the beginning of the age of freedom to Jesus' gift of himself. Little doubt, too, that his Galatian readers agreed with him.

Both benedictions and salutations establish that an understanding of origins is intrinsic to the identity of the Christian community. A central task of ministers is to clarify that identity by distinguishing the new age from the old, for it is essential to redemption (or any other word that Christians use to describe their new life) to understand the time before and the time after God's gracious gift in Christ. In a mysterious way, that transition is forever linked to the story of Jesus, with its terrible culmination in humiliation and exaltation. In that story Christians have discerned most acutely the collision between the two ages—one age in which good people seeking to serve God accomplished the most tragic rejection of God's love, and another age in which a rejected individual on a lonely cross opened the way to God's forgiveness and peace for all.

American Christians, however, do not find it congenial to think in terms of an inevitable conflict between two ages. We seldom visualize our daily desires and choices as the field for such conflict, and we need help if we are to recognize its signs. To recover this way of viewing the day's experiences, we may be instructed by an ancient Jewish writer, a contemporary of the New Testament church, for whom the idiom of two ages was entirely native: the writer of 2 Esdras. Esdras began with the recognition that the primary origin of the evil age should be traced to Adam's transgression against God's ordering of things: "The first Adam, burdened with an evil heart, transgressed and was overcome, as were also all who were descended from him. . . . The inhabitants of the city transgressed, in everything doing just as Adam and all his descendants had done, for they also had the evil heart" (3:21, 25–26; cf. 6:30; 7:11, 48). Esdras located the beginning of the old age in the evil heart of Adam, and he saw a universal extension of that heart in all "inhabitants of the city," in all of Adam's descendants (cf. Rom. 5:12).

The gravity of this universal extension occasioned despair on Esdras's part, as expressed in his dialogue with God (7:45–64). Here he confessed that the evil heart "has alienated us from God, and has brought us into corruption and the ways of death . . . and removed us far from life"(v. 48). "It would have been better if the dust itself had not been born. . . . We perish and we know it" (vv. 63–64). "Who

among the living is there that has not sinned?"(v. 46). His despair
leads to this revelation: "For this reason, the Most High has made not
one world but two" (v. 50). Thus the awareness of the evil age was
linked to an awareness of the prospect of another age, with the first
age "hurrying swiftly to its end" (4:26).

The Most High not only made two ages but also determined the
end of one and the beginning of the next: "When the Most High
made the world and Adam and all who have come from him, he *first*
prepared the judgment and the things that pertain to the judgment"
(7:70). In short, God's design from the beginning had included the
creation of both ages. The inauguration of the new age depended on
the maturation of that design. To understand the ending of one age
and the beginning of the other, one must recover the intentions of
God *before* the beginning of the first: "Then I planned these things,
and they were made through me alone and not through another;
just as the end shall come through me alone and not through another" (6:6).

What might one know about the intentions of the Most High before the beginning of the old age? Answers to such a question became
important to Esdras. He listed fourteen things that God planned "at
the beginning of the circle of the earth"; of these, seven are both typical and important:

> before the portals of the world were in place, and . . . before the
> foundations of paradise were laid, and . . . before the innumerable
> hosts of angels were gathered, and . . . before the footstool of Zion
> was established, and before the present years were reckoned, and
> before the imaginations of those who now sin were estranged, and
> before those who stored up treasures of faith were sealed.
>
> (6:1–5)

It is important in this connection to notice that Esdras was primarily
concerned with the need to recognize "the times of the Most High."
To him those times belonged to the Creator rather than to the creatures. As God's creation they were not historical ages to be measured
in centuries on a time line, like the age of the dinosaurs, for they tran-
scended such measurements. Nor did these times succeed one another seriatim, as the agricultural age succeeded the nomadic.
Rather, within a single human situation both times were present in
grace-laden signs and fearsome penalties, although few human ears
could detect the resonances that linked the hidden choices of human
hearts to the prevenient will of the Most High. To catch those resonances was an activity as elusive as it was vital.

When Esdras was speaking of such primal intentions, he was not seeking to escape from a dismal present into some distant realm of wistful nostalgia or wishful dream. His concern was to understand what was hidden in the bewildering confusions of the present. He found a key to the link between those confusions and the purposes of God: "Just as with everything that has occurred in the world, the beginning is evident, and the end manifest; so also are the times of the Most High. . . ." Esdras believed that every human situation and occurrence contains hidden within it a potential disclosure of both the beginning and the end of "the times of the Most High." But how does such a potential disclosure become real? ". . . so also are the times of the Most High: the beginnings are manifest in wonders and mighty works, and the end in penalties and in signs" (9:5–6). Wonders and mighty works give their evidence of the presence of the beginnings; penalties and signs give similar evidence of the presence of the end. Potentially, then, every present situation can disclose the end of one age in divine penalties and the beginning of another age in divine wonders. So the perception of God's primal and final purposes is inseparable from perceiving the signs of both ages within the present. The link is there, but only for those with eyes to see and ears to hear.

A modern analogy may be helpful here. In many hospitals the radiology laboratory has become a department of diagnostic imaging, where one of the advanced techniques is that of magnetic resonance imaging (MRI). For the purpose of examining the condition of internal organs, a magnetic field is set up within which resonances may be heard; with the help of a computer, those resonances then become images on a screen that enable the technician to determine the health or dysfunction of a particular organ. So scripture may be viewed as an example of spiritual MRI. Luke, for example, tells stories of Jesus that display a resonance between the mighty works of Jesus and perceptions of the new age, between the penalties Jesus announced and the judgment on the old age. Luke became conscious of some of these resonances when he reflected on Jesus' work in the light of the Genesis story of creation and the "evil heart" of Adam. One may observe a triangular magnetic field: the Genesis saga, the Gospel story, the ending of an old age and the beginning of a new. I examine first the story of Bethlehem shepherds, then the story of Mary, then the complex account of Jesus' work, and finally the work of his messengers. All four of these areas have significant resonances between Luke's understanding of Jesus, of Genesis, and of the collision and transition between old age and new.

The Story of the Shepherds

When one starts to read any literary work, what one finds depends in part on what one expects to find. In reading a Gospel, many modern readers expect to find the biography or life story of Jesus. In this case it is normal to look in the opening chapters for an account of his birth; accordingly these chapters are often called the birth story. But such an expectation can be misleading. Jesus' birth is described, to be sure, but only in a single verse (Luke 2:7); to this description are added such data as the time, the place, and the names of the parents. Yet such matters do not represent the central concern of the narrator or of his readers, for they already knew all this information. Rather, the chapters contain anticipations and announcements covering the entire story of God's involvement in everything that only began to happen in the days of Herod, that is, in all the events that are recounted in both volumes of Luke's authorship. One unfortunate result of such an expectation on the part of modern readers is that they restrict the use of these chapters to the Christmas season, missing what was central to Luke's intention. That intention was to provide, among other things, a series of messages of angels and songs of prophets that celebrated God's coming liberation of his people from their long captivity.

A second expectation is to suppose that Luke's concern was to provide a written history containing factual information in chronological sequence about the origins of the church. Such an expectation is equally misleading, for it results in a disappointment with the opening chapters and a tendency to skip over them in order to get to a more reliable narrative. In these opening chapters Luke gives more attention to the role of Gabriel than to any human actor. The prophecy of Simeon is far more significant than the identity of the Jewish king or the Roman governor. What we call "current events" do not appear on the stage. The night vision of unnamed shepherds is more important than the economic condition or social status of Jesus' family or the character of their home life in Nazareth. The divine purposes as conveyed by angels and prophets quite displaced the usual preoccupation with human plans and predicaments. For those who expect to find reliable data that satisfy twentieth-century expectations of history, these chapters can only diminish Luke's credibility as a historian. Few modern historians view them as helpful in reconstructing the actual events in Jesus' ministry.

What, then, should one expect to find in these chapters? For the two-volume work one cannot do better than to adopt the ancient titles:

The Gospel According to Luke, the Acts of the Apostles. But instead of the archaic term *gospel* one might better use the words of the angel: "the good news of great joy for all the people" (Luke 2:10). The opening chapters announce that news and trace those "acts" to their hidden origins. These chapters assume that the ultimate origin of such news and of such acts is found in "the Most High." The origin is variously traced to the Word *(logos)* of God, the Spirit *(pneuma)* of God, and the Power *(dynamis)* of God. All three are intrinsic to God's work of creation, whether in Genesis 1 or in Luke. The accepted agents for conveying this word are angels and prophets, who served as witnesses and servants of the word "from the beginning" (1:2; that phrase, *ap' archēs,* had multiple connotations in the archetypal thinking of the Bible). Each servant of the word, whether Gabriel or Elizabeth or Zechariah or Mary or Simeon or Anna, stressed the newness and the goodness of God's message. It was new because it stressed God's decision to replace his primeval curse with his blessing, his condemnation with his favor. It was good because it epitomized God's redemption and ransom offered for a people in captivity to the devil. Such liberation was ominously linked to "the falling and the rising of many in Israel" (2:34), when everyone would find in Jesus' work "occasions for stumbling" (17:1). If one expects to find in Luke's two-volume narrative the continuing impact of this news that was so good, one's reading of the opening chapters will be more in line with the evangelist's own understanding and intent.

Liberation is good to the degree that the prior captivity is onerous, as measured by its pain, its depth, its duration, and the manifest power of the captors. Great joy and great despair are true opposites. In these opening prophecies those opposites are suggested by a variety of idioms, all native to a distinctive language world. For example, Zechariah's song culminates in four images, all expressive of God's unexpected mercies: sin is replaced by forgiveness, darkness gives way to dawn, enmity is overcome by peace, death is mastered by life (1:77–79). Darkness, sin, enmity, death—these are precisely the results of God's condemnation of Adam, Eve, and their descendants.

Zechariah's song also gives a preview of all that follows. One sign of such planning is the editorial care in arranging a return to this beginning at the end of the Gospel, forming a significant *inclusio.* The initial assurance of forgiveness of sins (1:77) is repeated in Jesus' final instructions to the apostles (24:47). The coming of dawn following a night of sadness (1:78) finds a symbolic closure in the "dawn on the first day of the week," which in turn followed the darkness over the whole earth (23:44–46; 24:1). The prophet's anticipation of peace

(1:79) is fulfilled in Jesus' greeting to his disciples (24:36). Readers can conclude only that the same hand that crafted the opening of the Gospel crafted the closing.

But now it is time to turn to the four stories. Among the first to receive the announcement of God's blessings were shepherds doing their assigned nocturnal work!

> In that region there were shepherds living in the fields, keeping watch over their flock by night. Then an angel of the Lord stood before them, and the glory of the Lord shone around them, and they were terrified. But the angel said to them, "Do not be afraid; for see—I am bringing you good news of great joy for all the people: to you is born this day in the city of David a Savior, who is the Messiah, the Lord. This will be a sign for you: you will find a child wrapped in bands of cloth and lying in a manger." And suddenly there was with the angel a multitude of the heavenly host, praising God and saying,
>
> > "Glory to God in the highest heaven,
> > and on earth peace among those whom he favors!"
>
> When the angels had left them and gone into heaven, the shepherds said to one another, "Let us go now to Bethlehem and see this thing . . . which the Lord has made known to us." So they went with haste and found Mary and Joseph, and the child lying in the manger. When they saw this, they made known what had been told them about this child; and all who heard it were amazed at what the shepherds told them. But Mary treasured all these words and pondered them in her heart. The shepherds returned, glorifying and praising God for all they had heard and seen, as it had been told them. (Luke 2:8–20)

For modern readers who find it difficult to understand the story by reason of its cultural distance, one of its continuing functions is to invite them to enter into its own symbolic language world. That world is not so distant as to defy progress toward greater understanding if readers are amenable to adjusting their own expectations to the demands of the metaphorical language. Luke's first readers found it easier to respond to those demands than modern readers do, but there is no inherent reason why modern readers cannot respond to the images with improved comprehension.

Such progress is possible by moving in two directions. The first is to recall as fully as possible the social conditions faced by the community in which the story first circulated. This community was a group of Christian congregations in the eastern Mediterranean world during the second half of the first century. These congregations were Christian because they had become committed followers of a cruci-fied criminal known as the Messiah. Their loyalty was based on spe-cific knowledge of his work: his baptism, his prophetic messages to Israel, his debates with adversaries and instructions to disciples, his in-terpretation of the scriptures, his arrest, his trial, his death, his con-tinued presence through the Holy Spirit. Though their knowledge was no doubt partial and skewed, members of these congregations probably knew more about Jesus than modern readers of the Gospels can ever know. It was because of what they knew that they had risked their reputations, their fortunes, and even their lives. Their commit-ment to him had been sufficient both to arouse their faith and then to sustain them through violent confrontation with neighbors, both Jew and Gentile.

The costs of commitment to him would have shaped their re-sponses to reports they had heard. They would, for example, have re-called how Jesus had sent out his first follower-messengers as "lambs in the midst of wolves" (10:3). They would have listened with keen in-terest to the accounts of Jesus' battles with demons. Their own dan-gers would have made them fascinated with the hearings of Jesus before Caiaphas and Pilate and with the ways in which his predictions had come true that "the Son of Man must suffer." They would have known of the efforts of the authorities to keep the apostles from teaching "in the name of Jesus." Such communities of faith would have had great interest in the stories of the imprisonments of Peter, the lynching of Stephen, the execution of James. They had heard how Paul as a Pharisee had ravaged the churches, and how later, as a rep-resentative of Jesus, he had attracted the hatred of his former col-leagues. It is not at all impossible for modern readers to imagine themselves sharing this vulnerability of the first readers, subject to the same fear and cherishing the same memories. When they move in that direction, readers will be inclined to read the first chapters of Luke with the same kind of empathy that they read the last chapters.

A second direction in which one can move is to explore the dis-tinctive language used by those early Christians in expressing their memories and their faith. This language shaped the thought world of both the narrator and the first readers of the Gospel of Luke. This language not only made communication possible among them but also enabled the readers, on the basis of their own experience as Christians, to add depth to the words they read. The language that was native to them was composed in large part of a repertoire of metaphors and images inherited with the apostolic message itself.

This language estranged their adversaries in the same degree that it reinforced Christian solidarity with one another. The first contact with this language had no doubt come through the oral traditions transmitted by apostles, prophets, and teachers. Such traditions, in turn, were expressed largely in the language of the scriptures that were read regularly in synagogues and churches—the Law, the Prophets, and the Writings. But each use of scripture was subject to radically new interpretations under the impact of Jesus' own teaching and example. The appeal to scripture appears most clearly in the hundreds of quotations that punctuate the New Testament. But a far more pervasive influence may be detected in implicit allusions, in echoes and reverberations from familiar stories, in songs and prayers, pictures and parables, blessings and curses. Those idioms surfaced the well-traveled roads within the world of thought. Those who told the old, old stories could count on having listeners who lived in the same linguistic universe.

It is that language which confronts the reader of the opening chapters of Luke's Gospel, with accounts of three visits from angels. Such visits were commonly accepted as one way to bridge the distances between the invisible heaven and the visible earth. In the first of these visits the angel Gabriel came to the priest Zechariah as he was carrying out his duties in the temple. God's spokesman told him the good news that a son John would be born to him, one who would "make ready a people prepared for the Lord" (1:8–20). On a second trip Gabriel brought Mary the message that a son would be born to her, one to whom would be given the throne of his ancestor David. This son would come to be known as "the Son of God" (1:26–38). The third visit conveyed a double message. First a single angel, unnamed, announced to shepherds "the good news of great joy for all the people" in the birth of a savior in the city of David. Then a vast choir of angels joined in a soaring doxology, addressing their song to an audience both in heaven and earth: "Glory to God in the highest heaven, and on earth peace among those whom he favors" (2:14). It is this meeting of angels and shepherds that I want to examine. Who are these shepherds? Who are their listeners? Why the aura of awe and joy, of darkness and amazement, of mystery and miracle? What is this heavenly glory, this earthly peace, and how are they linked together? What kind of language is this? In what kind of world does it belong?

The initial audience of the angels is made up of shepherds, unnamed and unnumbered. They are clearly selected as representatives of, and potential messengers to, "all the people." That phrase may be better translated as "the whole people"; in Luke the phrase is often used in speaking of Israel as a whole. The shepherds do, in fact, fulfill this assignment by telling what had happened so that "all who heard it were amazed" (v. 18). As is common in the Bible, the hierophany utilized a distinctive language, conveying a special word from a particular God to the elect people by way of special messengers, first angelic and then human. The news was sung, not spoken; and the act of singing signaled a radical change in the situation, first in heaven and then on earth. To convey this change to the intended audience, the shepherds had been chosen by God. On completing their assignment, the shepherds left the stage and did not appear again.

Surely the narrator's choice of shepherds was not accidental. More than weavers or potters, shepherds had played a central role in many biblical dramas. Both as a noun and as a verb the term "shepherd" had proved useful in many different situations for many different audiences. The basic literal reference was to men whose regular occupation was feeding, guiding, and guarding flocks of sheep and goats. A derived metaphor often referred to kings charged with defending and governing a city or nation. Biblical histories presented a long roster of people who were called shepherds, and in most of these cases the metaphorical use had displaced the literal. The first shepherd was Abel, whose death at the hands of his brother guaranteed him a place in later annals. His death came to provide an important contrast to the death of Jesus (e.g., Heb. 12:24). In the patriarchal legends about the time when famine forced Israel to migrate to Egypt, Joseph introduced his eleven brothers as shepherds (Gen. 46:32). In the succession of heroes in Israel, David first appears on the scene as a shepherd, and even after his accession as king he continued to be revered as the shepherd of Israel. His successors, whether as kings, prophets, or poets, inherited his figurative role. A respected idiom visualized God addressing current leaders of Israel as shepherds, even when they were betraying that vocation (Ezek. 34:1ff.). In contrast to a long period of such betrayals, God had promised a renewal of the covenant in terms of shepherds and flocks in the land of Benjamin: "in this place that is waste . . . there shall again be pasture for shepherds resting their flocks. In the towns of the hill country . . . the land of Benjamin . . . flocks shall again pass under the hands of the one who counts them, says the LORD" (Jer. 33:12–13). In texts like this, the metaphorical connotations have displaced the literal denotations.

This figuration took on even more complex shapes after the image came to be used for God in the role as shepherd and ruler of Israel. The double metaphor of shepherd/flock came to suggest many of

the subtler components of the bond between the Deity and the people, between heaven and earth, the invisible and the visible. Among
Christians, many of these same components came to be applied to
Jesus as "the good shepherd" who "counted" all his sheep and knew
them all by name (John 10).

Over preceding centuries this idiom had helped to give shape to
an entire symbolic universe. It may help modern readers to enter that
universe if they look for the boundaries between three contiguous
realms. One is the visible realm where people carried on their daily
activities of sleeping and waking, playing and working, loving and hat-
ing. In this realm the term "shepherd" referred simply to one of many
ordinary human occupations, no more and no less. A second is the
imagined realm within which the human community visualized itself
as a flock of sheep, cared for by God as the great shepherd who was
ultimately responsible for its formation and care. This chief shepherd
appointed shepherds to govern and guide the flock. Opposed to this
second was a third realm, also imagined but also real, in which a community lived that had become estranged from the great shepherd because it had been deceived into following false shepherds into a
wilderness where it had become prey to the wild beasts of the earth.
In this realm the true God had been replaced by other gods, so that
Israel had ceased to be his flock.

In the first of these three realms, to assign important figurative
roles to shepherds would be wrong, however important they may have
been to the economy. By contrast, in the two imagined realms, to sub-
stitute the literal work of shepherds in the first realm for their figurative role in these realms would cause great confusion. Luke was not
concerned, at least here, with the wages or living conditions of shepherds in the Judea of his day; but both author and readers were
greatly concerned with Jesus' messengers in whose work the boundaries of the three worlds were disclosed.

The interaction of these three realms may be illustrated by the
Matthean version of the Lord's Prayer (6:9–13, NRSV). The two petitions in the center bring into expression the simple immediate needs
for daily bread and for the resolution of human animosities. The first
three petitions, however, recognize the priority of the Father's action
in one invisible realm—his holiness, his kingdom, his will. So, too, the
last two petitions visualize the third realm where the evil one is lord
and the potential source of a dreaded time of trial. It is from his captivity that the Father has the power to rescue his children.

As a daily prayer, these petitions presuppose the priority of the two
invisible realms and the constant interaction of all three. They also

presuppose the basic attitude toward the two ages or kingdoms: the struggle with evil in the present age, the need for divine help for the gift of a new age, and the urgent hope for such a gift. Such help is requested not through immediate economic or political changes but through the experience of an ending and a beginning in the imagined realms whose priority is recognized by the prayer (e.g., below, pages 120–24). Such recognition, however, is quite absent from the minds of those who repeat the mantra thoughtlessly. They often live in a narrow world described by Annie Dillard: "It is a fault of infinity to be too small to find. . . . No rift between one note of the chorus and the next opens on infinity." Dillard visualized members of a choir singing one note of the music after another, and finding that infinity is too small to appear between the C-sharp and the following B-flat in an anthem. Or again: "It is a fault of eternity to be crowded out by time. . . . No spear of eternity interposes itself between work and lunch."[2] Work is so demanding that it permits no time to reckon with the presence of the Eternal in either the job or the food. By contrast, Jesus' prayer assumes that the only significant context for either work or lunch is furnished by reverence for the Divine and escape from the demonic. For him, lunch is interposed between recognition of God's will and fear of the devil's deceits.

But I must return to Luke's story with its picture of the intrusion of the infinite into the nocturnal routine of the shepherds. As already noted, their role was central in the imagined worlds of both the narrator and his readers. Who could provide a more fitting audience than the shepherds for the angelic announcement of the birth of a great Shepherd? What language would be more fitting than the language of scripture? I want now to examine the scriptural source of that language. (In speaking of scripture, I have in mind the Hebrew scriptures, which in the time of the early church were the only scriptures of Christians.)

In two texts Luke's points of contact with previous traditions are so substantial and so numerous as to merit major consideration. One of these texts links Luke to the Greek translation of Ezekiel 34:23ff. First, one should notice the identification of a specific shepherd who receives a specific assignment:

> I will raise up *[anastēsō]* over them one shepherd,
>   my slave David.
> He will feed them *[poimainō]*;
> He will be their shepherd *[poimēn]*
> And I, the Lord, will be their God;
> And in their midst my slave David will be their ruler.
>   (34:23–24, LXX, my trans.)

As mentioned, "shepherd" was, in Christian parlance, a basic image for both God and Christ. In that same parlance, the verb to raise up (anastēsō) was used to refer to God's action in the resurrection from the dead of the son of David, the shepherd, whose work was to reestablish the kingdom of David as an eternal kingdom. Also in the New Testament the term "slave" was used to establish Jesus' qualification to rule (Phil. 2:7); it was the same term used of David in Ezekiel. Accordingly, when Christians heard Ezekiel 34 being read as scripture, they would respond to those words as a promise that God had fulfilled in the slavery and enthronement of Jesus. Loyalty to their Lord would have prepared them to apply to Jesus the continuing promise of God in Ezekiel 34:

> I will make with David a covenant of peace: I will banish evil wild beasts from the earth. They will make their homes in the wilderness and sleep securely. I will give them a dwelling place in a circle around my mountain. I will give you rain, a shower of blessing. The trees in the plain will yield their fruit; The earth will yield its strength. They will make their homes on the earth in hope of peace. . . . No longer will the wild beasts of the earth devour them. . . . I will raise up for them a plant of peace. No longer will they be destroyed by famine on the earth. . . . They will know that I am the Lord, their God, and they are my people, the house of Israel. . . . You are my sheep, the sheep of my flock, and I am your God, the Lord.   (Ezek. 34:25–31, LXX, my trans.)

Comparing Ezekiel's prophecy with Luke's story, one finds that the two symbolic worlds were entirely congenial. Both texts speak of a world in which God is the ultimate source of saving action: "I will make . . . will give . . . will banish . . . will raise up." Both reflect a universe in which God's immediate concern was the destiny of Israel: "my people . . . my sheep . . . my flock . . . the house of David." In both worlds, shepherds were God-appointed guardians and messengers, responsible to the ultimate Shepherd for the care of this flock.

Significant details include the strong accent on the promise of peace on earth. The word "peace" appears three times and has many cognate terms: home, security, harvest, hope, shower of blessing. Peace connoted all of these terms. The word "earth" appears five times, again with a large constellation of images: wilderness, mountain, plain, wild beasts, famine, captivity. In Ezekiel, the gift of peace included "a shower of blessing" (eulogia); in Luke it brought God's "favor" (eudokia); those two words are virtually synonymous ways of describing the termination of God's curse on Adam and his descendants. In Ezekiel's case this action marked deliverance from famine, from captivity, from vulnerability to the wild beasts of the earth. Peace on earth was an image that summarized the whole range of blessings that could supplant this wide range of deprivations.

This summary should make one thing clear: a congregation of Christians whose mind was acclimated to the language of Ezekiel would have felt at home in the world of Luke's thought; they would have understood the angel's announcement of peace on earth as a fulfillment of God's promise to Ezekiel. The two worlds had the same horizons, the same latitude and longitude, the same gravitation laws. Neither Ezekiel nor Luke described social conditions in ways that would invite statistical measurement of such matters as income levels. Their sense of God's blessing was not dependent on immediate prospects of economic prosperity. The struggle between shepherds and wild beasts could not easily be translated into current battles between economic classes or political sects. Those conflicts may have been bitter, but the symbolic language concealed the identity of the opposing groups. Human choices determined ultimate destinies, but those destinies were hidden behind the two alternatives of peace on earth or continued warfare with wild beasts.

A second text provides background for Luke's thought, a text suggested by Ezekiel's image of peace, for Ezekiel's prophecy echoed the Genesis story of God's curses on Adam and Eve, on their eldest son, on the earth, and on one of the wild beasts, the crafty serpent. The Genesis story of those curses provided the foil for the prophet's assurance of their removal. Consider several contrasts:

> THE CURSE: When you till the earth it will no longer yield to you its strength   (Gen. 4:12)
> THE BLESSING: The earth will yield its strength
> (Ezek. 34:27, LXX, my trans.)

Ezekiel's cancellation of the curse used virtually the same words.

> THE CURSE: Cursed is the earth because of you; in toil you shall eat of it all the days of your life; thorns and thistles it shall bring forth for you   (Gen. 3:17–18)
> THE BLESSING: The trees in the plain will yield their fruit
> (Ezek. 34:37, LXX, my trans.)

The sterility of the earth, with continued frustrations of the farmer's work, will be replaced by fertility and plenty.

THE CURSE: Cursed are you . . . among all wild creatures *[thēria]*. I will put enmity between you and the woman, and between your offspring and hers (Gen. 3:14–15)
THE BLESSING: I will banish evil wild beasts *[thēria]* from the earth. . . . No longer will the wild beasts of the earth devour them
(Ezek. 34:25, 28, LXX)

God's curse on the serpent, the craftiest of the wild beasts on the earth, was clearly in Ezekiel's mind when he shaped his pictures of peace on the earth.

THE CURSE: You shall eat the plants of the field (Gen. 3:18)
THE BLESSING: No longer will they be destroyed by famine on the earth (Ezek. 34:29)

THE CURSE: You will be a fugitive and a wanderer on the earth
(Gen. 4:12)
THE BLESSING: They will make their homes in the wilderness and sleep securely. . . . They will make their homes on the earth in hope of peace (Ezek. 34:25, 27)

The whole range of curses against the serpent, against Adam and Eve and Cain, and against the earth came into view in Ezekiel, providing the canvas on which the prophet painted his picture of peace. In both curses and blessings, the reference to the earth is central. To Ezekiel it was essential that the fulfillment of God's promises to David would include a removal of the primordial curses. Just as the Genesis saga of the initial penalties for human sin shaped the thought world of Ezekiel, so the thought world of Ezekiel helped to shape the thought world of Luke.

One is prompted then to ask concerning possible direct intertextual resonance between Genesis and Luke. Having gauged the associations between Ezekiel's promise of peace and Luke's, and having seen the links between Ezekiel's views of the antithesis of peace and that of Genesis, can one posit any direct link between Genesis and Luke? Is there independent evidence of Luke's awareness of the curse of Cain and of its relevance to the story Luke was telling? The answer is positive. Consider first God's rebuke to Cain:

Listen! *Your brother's blood* is crying out to me from the earth . . . which has opened its mouth to receive your brother's blood from your hand. When you till the earth it will no longer yield to you its strength. (Gen. 4:10–11)

Now consider this word from Jesus as reported by Luke. It is a quotation from "the Wisdom of God" in which God said:

> I will send them prophets and apostles, some of whom they will kill and persecute, so that this generation may be charged with the blood of all the prophets shed since the foundation of the world, from *the blood of Abel* to the blood of Zechariah. . . . Yes, I tell you, it will be charged against this generation."   (Luke 11:49–51)

To Jesus, and presumably also to Luke, the curse on the first murderer was no vague, distant recollection of a biblical text but a current reality, as inescapable as the conflicts between Jesus as the shepherd son of David and the Pharisees as the recognized shepherds of Israel. The blood of Abel, swallowed by the earth, was still crying out with the guilt of all generations of fratricidal violence. When Luke looked back from the time that he was writing the story, that blood included the blood of Jesus himself, as well as the blood of apostles, sent out by Jesus to announce God's mercy to Jesus' own murderers. Luke and his readers had drunk "the new covenant in my blood" (22:20); they knew well the price of peace on earth, paid by this shepherd for these very enemies. For Christians, this peace and this blood were inseparable images of liberation.

Readers of Luke would see the kaleidoscope of pictures triggered by the text of Genesis: Abel as a shepherd and his murder, the true and false shepherds as described in Ezekiel 34, the Bethlehem shepherds guarding their flock by night, the good shepherd giving his life for his flock, the pastors and bishops in Luke's churches undergoing bitter and massive persecution. Earth, blood, night, wild beasts, heaven, angels, shepherds—within this narrative world, the assurance of Jesus seems to be almost an echo of the angel's song of peace on earth: "Do not be afraid, little flock, for it is your Father's good pleasure to give you the kingdom" (Luke 12:32). To address the flock in these words presupposes that the speaker was himself their shepherd.

Such an assurance by Jesus is adequate evidence that to Luke the shepherd Abel and the shepherds in the field outside Bethlehem had many successors. But still further evidence is in Luke's version of the farewell address given by Paul to the elders of the church in Ephesus. Paul was bound for Jerusalem where, as he was warned by the Holy Spirit, imprisonment and persecution were waiting. These elders would never see his face again. So Paul took the opportunity to prepare them for coming tests:

> Keep watch over yourselves and over all the flock, of which the Holy Spirit has made you overseers, to shepherd the church of God that he obtained with the blood of his Son. I know that after I have gone, savage wolves will come in among you, not sparing the flock.

> Some even from your own group will come distorting the truth in
> order to entice the disciples to follow them.   (Acts 20:28–30)

Holy Spirit, shepherds, flock—these images are central to Luke 2.
The blood of Jesus, the blood of Paul and of the Ephesian elders—
the blood shed since the foundation of the world—that blood was the
means by which these shepherds gave their witness to "the good news
of God's grace" (Acts 20:24), a message for which the angel's announcement in Luke 2 provided the necessary divine prelude in the
imagined world of Luke.

Now one may recall the adage: "Imagine the past; remember the
future." Like all adages, this one has many potential meanings, each
depending on a particular context. In the context of Luke's message
from the angels, the future that was remembered was the future of
Jesus, Stephen, James, Paul, Ephesian elders. The past that was imagined was a world of angels singing the doxology and announcing
peace on earth among those whom God favors. The story of the shepherds was a prototype of many subsequent stories.

The answers to two questions should be evident by now. First, who
are the shepherds in Luke's imagined world? They are the imagined
descendants of Abel and David and those given God's promise in
Ezekiel 34. They are imagined prototypes of Jesus, Peter, Paul, the elders of the Ephesian church. They are chosen to receive a revelation
of God's prior action and to deliver that message of "great joy for all
the people," joy befitting the gift of a new age of blessedness into an
old age of alienation. This divine paradigm will decisively shape the
future.

Second, what is the peace they are instructed to proclaim? It is a
peace that comes on earth among those whom God favors with the
new creation (of Word, Spirit, Power). It is the peace to be won by the
Son of Man who is son of David. The promised blessedness included
God's lifting of the curse on the serpent and the earth, on Eve and
Adam and their progeny, a curse that had taken many forms since the
expulsion from Eden. A sign of this peace was given to the shepherds:
"a child . . . lying in a manger."

That sign anticipated all that the son of David would do in his
earthly work. It was followed near the end of Luke's Gospel by another sign that reflected all that the son of David had done. He had
brought peace to earth by casting out demons, by healing the sick, by
feeding the hungry, by freeing the captives, and by raising the dead.
Thus his followers, as he entered Jerusalem for the final struggle,
"began to praise God joyfully with a loud noise for all the deeds of
power that they had seen" (19:37). The words of their doxology

(19:38) were deftly shaped as a counterpart (a choral *inclusio*) to the doxology of the angels in chapter 2: "Blessed is the king who comes in the name of the Lord." So far the words are a quotation from scripture (Zech. 9:9), for which Luke was probably indebted to Mark (Mark 11:9).

The response of the Pharisees was immediate. They urged Jesus: "order your disciples to stop." They saw this praise as blasphemy against God. Their blindness was identical with Jerusalem's. They did not recognize "the things that *make for peace.*" Peace had been offered; peace had been rejected. In response to that blindness Jesus wept over the city (Luke 19:41).

Luke added to the doxology two lines of his own, and carefully chosen lines they were: "Peace in heaven, and glory in the highest heaven." The variations from the doxology in chapter 2 are obvious. There the singers had been angels; here they are the disciples. There the audience had been shepherds; here heaven. There angels announced the coming fulfillment of God's promises in Ezekiel 34; here the disciples announced the coming fulfillment of God's promise in Zechariah. There the sign had been a helpless infant; here a man from Galilee riding a borrowed donkey. There the peace had been on earth; here in heaven. There the order had been first glory, then peace; here first peace, then glory.

Why the changes? I believe the answer lies in the changed situation. In Bethlehem the angels announced Jesus' mission *before* it was to begin; in Jerusalem, in the strange sign of a king entering his capital city riding on a donkey, his disciples announced Jesus' final struggle with the evil one, the outcome of which would be Satan's fall from heaven (cf. Rev. 12:7–12). The glorification of God would accompany *this* peace in heaven. Of course, that peace was linked to the peace on earth, the winning of which led to the glorification of God on earth. Viewed thus, the inner logic of the birth story with its sign is completed in the inner logic of the passion story with its sign—the power of God made manifest in human weakness. In telling the story of the shepherds, Luke was quite aware of that logic.

Viewed thus, the story of the Bethlehem shepherds has an inner logic that vindicates its integrity. These shepherds do not reappear in Luke's later instructions to Theophilus. They leave the stage in Luke 2:20 with their mission completed, for that mission was a symbolic one. In one sense the two-volume work describes the delivery of their message "for the whole people." In another sense, whenever an early congregation joined in their song (for the doxology was sung) the congregation took the place of the army of angels. Perhaps that is ample reason why poets and composers have often been excellent interpreters of Luke, as, for example, Johann Rist:

> Break forth, O beauteous heavenly light
> And usher in the morning.
> Ye shepherds shrink not with affright
> But heed the angel's warning.
> This child now weak in infancy
> Our confidence and joy shall be,
> The power of Satan breaking,
> And peace eternal making.[3]

The Story of Mary

In the sixth month the angel Gabriel was sent by God to a town in Galilee called Nazareth, to a virgin engaged to a man whose name was Joseph, of the house of David. The virgin's name was Mary. And he came to her and said, "Greetings, favored one! The Lord is with you." But she was much perplexed by his words and pondered what sort of greeting this might be. The angel said to her, "Do not be afraid, Mary, for you have found favor with God. And now, you will conceive in your womb and bear a son, and you will name him Jesus. He will be great, and will be called the Son of the Most High, and the Lord God will give him the throne of his ancestor David. He will reign over the house of Jacob forever, and of his kingdom there will be no end." Mary said to the angel. "How can this be, since I am a virgin?" The angel said to her, "The Holy Spirit will come upon you, and the power of the Most High will overshadow you; therefore the child to be born will be holy; he will be called Son of God." Then Mary said, "Here am I, the servant of the Lord; let it be with me according to your word." Then the angel departed from her. (Luke 1:26–38)

In the account of the shepherds I suggested subtle influences that possibly issued from the Genesis saga; one may now search for similar influences in the story of Mary, though their presence is not a foregone conclusion. One should certainly recognize in advance that a great variety of factors must have been present in the gestation of the tradition. Oral traditions are more susceptible to such influences than written traditions, because once a story is written, the text discourages alterations. But, in the case of oral reminiscence, at each retelling both the narrator and the listeners may readily add details: allusions to scripture, echoes of Christian hymns, references to current legends, new images and analogies. When an interpreter detects an intertextual link, one should take caution to avoid exaggeration of its importance in shaping the narrative. At every stage of development, multiple motifs are at work, and nothing is easier than to simplify an extremely complex process. Even so, some exaggeration may at times be useful in calling attention to submerged connections; a lie may help, as my colleague Paul Schubert used to say, to uncover the truth.

In the case of Mary, many interpreters have sensed that her portrait was painted to show likeness and unlikeness to the picture of Eve. One of these interpreters was John Milton. He pictured the archangel addressing Eve thus: "Hail! Mother of mankind, whose fruitful womb shall fill the world more numerous with thy sons." Then the poet spoke of this "Hail!" as "the holy salutation used long after to blest Mary, second Eve."[4] In the stories of both Eve and Mary, it is God who takes the initiative. In both, God creates human beings in his image and calls the result good. In both, God's word is assumed to provide the initial impulse: "Let it be with me according to your *word*" (Luke 1:38). God chooses through each woman to influence all later generations; the results of his influence are visualized as having no end. To speak of either woman is to use a symbol of universality and creativity. In the case of both mothers, the birth of a first son is of high importance. Through those sons, many generations of descendants are "foreknown"; those descendants are thought to have their existence *in* their mothers; through them the mothers share *in* the life of all succeeding generations. Both women received God's blessing, at least at the outset, and that blessing carried far-reaching significance, because it augured for them and their descendants some kind of dominion over the earth. In both lines of descent, life and death were at stake, outcomes depending simultaneously on God's arm and on human decision. Both stories revealed the boundaries between the visible and the imagined realms.

The stories reflect a kind of thinking that one can call "Alpha-time thinking" since it assumes so much is determined by the first event in a series. The earlier an event, the more authoritative and decisive. Primal archetypes exert permanent influence over a vast range of outcomes. Stories of beginnings do not become more and more distant with the passing of time, but more and more determinative of present conflicts and choices. Looking back from the present, people recognize the power and purpose of God in the primal moment. This kind of thinking permeated the Christian images of both Eve and Mary.

The contrasts between the two mothers were even more significant than the similarities; it is those contrasts that are essential to the

Lukan story. Unlike Eve, Mary was a virgin. Unlike Eve's first son, the murderer, Mary's son was savior of the world. Unlike Cain, Mary's son was conceived by an intervention of the Holy Spirit, so that, according to Alpha-time thinking, this son could claim primacy in God's ordering of things. More specifically, one may distinguish between the two mothers by noting four points in their two stories: the character of the tests, their reactions to the tests, the immediate results, and God's final verdicts.

Eve's testing had been prompted by a word of God that contained both a permission and a prohibition: "You may freely eat of every tree of the garden; but of the tree of the knowledge of good and evil you shall not eat, for in the day that you eat of it you shall die" (Gen. 2:16–17). Eve accepted God's permission without a second thought, but not the prohibition; that prohibition offered the serpent an opportunity to suggest both doubt and denial: "You will not die." He supported that denial with a plausible explanation of why God had issued the ban: "God knows that when you eat of it your eyes will be opened, and you will be like God, knowing good and evil" (3:4–5). Left to decide whether to trust the serpent's lie or God's ban, Eve chose the lie.

One should not pass hastily over the contradiction between the promises of the two invisible adversaries. God said "You shall die" and the serpent, "You will not die." That contradiction was what gave to Eve's choice its ultimate seriousness. Yet she and Adam did not die on the day when they ate the fruit, for Genesis records later on that at his death Adam was more than nine hundred years old (5:5). It would seem that God's threat was empty and the serpent's lie the truth— unless different definitions of death were involved. And that was surely the case. The issue posed by Eve's choice was which definition of death she should accept, God's or the serpent's. The Genesis epic implies that she and Adam did die in some sense on the day they chose to challenge God's ban. That being true, her decision reflected the power of both the serpent and God in that invisible world controlled by each.

What, now, was the character of the test that Mary faced? God's word also placed her in the position of making a fateful choice: "The Lord is with you. . . . Do not be afraid. . . . You have found favor with God. Listen! You will conceive in your womb and bear a son. . . . He will be great and will be called the Son of the Most High" (Luke 1:28–33, my trans.). Perplexed by this message, Mary could not fathom "what sort of greeting this might be." Gabriel's injunction not to be afraid implied the possibility of fear and, with fear, the possibility of not accepting so incredible and daunting a disclosure. The message surely gave ample room for suspicion: "How can this be?" Mary had as much reason to doubt the divine word as had Eve. Indeed, the story assumes that the temptation to do so was very strong; yet the text makes no mention of the presence or intervention of the serpent. Did Mary allow him less of an opportunity? Or was Ignatius's explanation of his absence correct? "The virginity of Mary, and her giving birth, were hidden from the Prince of this world, as was also the death of the Lord" (*Letter to the Ephesians* 19.1; cf. 1 Cor. 2:8, K. Lake trans.). So much for the character of the testing of the two mothers.

Their immediate reactions to the two tests are well known. In Eve's case, the forbidden fruit offered a triple attraction: "The woman saw that the tree was good for food, and that it was a delight to the eyes, and that the tree was to be desired to make one wise" (Gen. 3:6). One can readily understand the magnetic attraction of these three things, for they are desired by every person. Wisdom, beauty, food—all are undoubtedly good and all are necessary for human survival. Yet God had said no. Eve's reaction was open and flagrant disobedience: "She took of the fruit and ate." At the instigation of the serpent, she assumed that God's ban had been based on the effort to protect God's own jurisdiction. But it was her own self-interest that made her vulnerable to the serpent's craftiness.

The reaction of Mary to the divine word could hardly have differed more from that of Eve: "See! I am a slave of the Lord. Let everything happen to me according to your word" (Luke 1:38, my trans.). Here one detects the unconditional self-humiliation of a slave before her imperious Lord. Here is the unreserved acceptance of a promise even before she could fully understand it: "A slave of the Lord." The word "slave" is preferable to the usual translation "servant" as both more accurate and more attuned to the context. Here it is paired with its twin metaphor "lord"; the lord and the slave are bound by a strong relationship of command and obedience, ownership and being owned. Such is not the relationship conveyed by the weaker term "servant" as used in the American expression "service economy." "Slave" is also more compatible with Mary's humiliation *(tapeinosis);* it provides a more vivid antithesis to the subsequent blessedness (a similar antithesis occurs in the Philippian hymn regarding the slavery and lordship of Jesus, Philippians 2). Mary's slavery links her closely to the meek and lowly folk of the Magnificat and sets her apart from the proud and wealthy (Luke 1:51–53). Her self-humiliation in accepting the Lord's word is a clear anticipation of the mission of her son, who would become last of all and slave of all.

The immediate results of the two decisions were expressed in diverse images. On eating the fruit, Eve and her husband came, as God had warned, to a new knowledge of good and evil. That knowledge opened their eyes to their own nakedness before God, so they took desperate steps to hide from him (Gen. 3:8). This nakedness has often been interpreted as a symbol of puritanical morality, as if human nakedness were in itself sinful. In Genesis, however, nakedness symbolized not the sinfulness of sex, but the vulnerability of being in the wrong before God. Eve and Adam did not want to face God without the protection of clothing; hence, the picture of them skulking through the underbrush, fearful of being caught in flagrant disobedience. Their nakedness symbolized their helplessness; they had no excuse that would stand up in God's eyes. (Christian uses of the symbol of nakedness may be found in Mark 14:51–52; John 21:7; Acts 19:16; 2 Cor. 5:1–5; Heb. 4:13; Rev. 3:17–18; 16:15.) As God had warned, on the day of their sin (Gen. 2:17) they did, in fact, lose their access to the tree of life (Gen. 3:24).

God's testing of Mary yielded a quite different result. God had no need to search for her; he was with her, assuring her of his favor. In her blessedness she would conceive and bear a son who would himself be a blessing and a source of blessing. Gabriel's promise would be confirmed by the descent of the Holy Spirit and by the power of the Most High, gifts that made possible many later acts of the Spirit and works of power. As the Spirit said through Elizabeth, "Blessed are you among women, and blessed is the fruit of your womb" (Luke 1:42). This double blessing was the precise opposite of the curse on Eve; it was, however, like the curse in that it was extended to cover the firstborn son. In fact, the chief concern of both blessing and curse was the future of the two lines of descent. One seriously underestimates the importance that Luke attached to this blessing of Mary unless one discerns in it God's reversal of the curse on Eve, who, one should recall, was "the mother of all living" (Gen. 3:20).

The glimpse of the whole future formed the climax of both stories. In the case of the first mother, God included her with the serpent in the first curse: "I will put enmity between you and the woman, and between your offspring and hers" (Gen. 3:15). Eve experienced the full force of that enmity, as did her firstborn son, along with all who inherited their cycle of violence. Early Christians had good reason to remember that curse, because, as the Lord's Prayer reminded them, the same enmity was turned against them.

But such enmity was conspicuous by its absence from Luke's picture of Mary; he made no mention of the serpent or of his many aliases. Instead of enmity, the fullness of God's blessing was repeated over and over. In subsequent chapters, readers find everywhere the signs of enmity between her son and the devil, but Mary's own total obedience to Gabriel seems to have freed her from the curse on Eve.

The author of 4 Maccabees told of another virgin whose children brought redemption to Israel. This woman was the mother of the seven sons who courageously welcomed tortures and martyrdom for the sake of Israel. She proved to be "more noble than males in stead-fastness" (4 Macc. 15:30). In her case, virginity took the form of re-pelling "the deceitful serpent": "I was a pure virgin and did not go outside my father's house; but I guarded the rib from which woman was made. No seducer corrupted me on a desert plain, nor did the de-stroyer, the deceitful serpent, defile the purity of my virginity. In the time of my maturity I remained with my husband" (18:6–9).

Luke agreed with the author of 4 Maccabees in associating virgin-ity with purity, with courage, and with the redemption of Israel, though he did not refer in the Gospel to seduction by the serpent. Likewise, Mary seems to be unaware of the prospect of public shame that would fall on her with the birth of a bastard son. Such shame was clearly a factor in the Matthean drama. Even more emphatic was the version of the story in an apocryphal gospel. There, when Joseph heard of Mary's pregnancy, he shouted, "Who has deceived me? Who has done this evil in my house and defiled her? Has the story (of Adam) been repeated in me? For as Adam was (absent) in the hour of his prayer and the serpent came and found Eve alone and seduced and defiled her, so also has it happened to me" (*Protoevangelium of James*, 13.1, trans. R. McL. Wilson). No intimation of such seduction appears in Luke. It would seem that Mary's humble obedience was so complete as to provide immunity to the serpent's lies (cf. also *Diogne-tus* 12.7–8).

In Genesis a second curse was levied on Eve alone: "I will greatly increase your pangs in bearing children; with terrible travail will you bring them forth" (3:16, LXX, my trans.). The Hebrew text used the strongest possible idiom to convey the severity of this curse as a legacy that Eve shared with her female descendants, but the account of Jesus' birth has no suggestion of "terrible travail." Gabriel said simply, "You will bear a son," and when Jesus was born, Luke gave more at-tention to the problem of finding lodging in Bethlehem than to any birth pangs. Mary seems to have been wholly free of Eve's legacy. Ar-guments from silence are notoriously weak, but one should not ig-nore this contrast between the two mothers. This possibility is supported by a text in Isaiah, a book Luke often cites. One of the

signs to Isaiah of God's vindication of Zion would be God's miraculous opening of Zion's womb: "Before she was in labor she gave birth;
before her pain came upon her she delivered a son" (Isa. 66:7–9). To
Isaiah such a delivery was an unheard-of mystery; it would provide
ample cause for joy among all who loved Jerusalem. The lifting of the
curse that God had declared in Genesis 3 would be a sure sign of salvation; in effect, a return to the situation in Eden before the mother
of all succumbed to the lies of the serpent. Thus Luke apparently
agreed with Isaiah in viewing a painless childbirth as God's offer of
salvation through a second Eve.

In Genesis God used a third way of penalizing Eve for her disobedience: "Your desire shall be for your husband, and he shall rule over
you" (Gen. 3:16). This text explained the long history of marital suf-
ferings as being a result of God's punishment of the primal sin. The
tragic actuality of marriage as a form of slavery was attributed simultaneously to the wife's sexual passion and the husband's masculine
domination. It is important to remember that this marital captivity
was treated not as sin but as God's condemnation of earlier sin. This
story does not place the accent on the sinful character of sexual intercourse but on God's punishment of Eve for succumbing to the serpent's appeal to her self-interest, her desire for wisdom, beauty, and
food. The text does not justify either uninhibited sexual passion or
masculine chauvinism; rather, it is a way of describing Eve's legacy as
a form of God's curse on her for defying his warning.

The story of Mary is that of a woman free of this legacy. God's
favor comes to her when she is still "a virgin engaged to a man whose
name was Joseph" (Luke 1:27). At the outset of the story this fact of
virginity is mentioned twice. It seems to be stressed also in Mary's
reply to the angel: "How can this be, since I am a virgin?" (1:34).
Though this use of an English idiom can be defended, the Greek
text, translated more literally, reads: "How can this be, since I do not
know [i.e., since I have had no sexual intercourse with] a husband?"
Not only is this translation more literal, but it also preserves the
metaphorical overtones of the original curse. Genesis 4:1 reads, for
example, "Adam *knew* his wife," and the wording of the curse reads,
"your desire [sexual passion] shall be for your *husband*" (3:16). It is
therefore quite possible to interpret the references to Mary's virginity as a way of indicating her freedom from Eve's curse. Unlike Eve,
Mary was not yet in a position of being subject to sexual passion for
a husband or of being bound to obey his commands. The birth of
this child was to be traced instead to conception by the Holy Spirit,
a new creation through the Spirit, the Word, and the Power of God.

Thus God's blessing on her and her child supplanted his specific curse of Eve and her offspring.

This way of understanding Mary's virginity as a form of narrative theology that stresses the reality of a new creation is supported by the shift in emphasis within Mary's own song of praise. That song begins with a recognition of God's favor on "the humiliation of his slave," but it soon turns to poetic summaries of the many ways in which God has fulfilled "the promise made to our ancestors." It was in the fulfillment of that promise that Luke's readers discerned the ultimate miracle. The song, like the story, celebrates the reality of a new beginning and an amnesty for the primeval sins that provoked the primeval curses. In the development of the oral tradition, this song may well have provided the original nucleus around which the narrative of Jesus' birth took its final shape, after having been sung over and over by many beneficiaries of that new beginning.

In support of the inclusion of God's people in the blessing of Mary is the fact that scripture had many times referred to Zion or Israel as God's virgin daughter, often with a condemnation of frequent whoredoms. Typical of the condemnations is Jeremiah 18:13: "Thus says the LORD: Ask among the nations: Who has heard the like of this? The *virgin* Israel has done a most horrible thing." Typical also is this promise: "Thus says the LORD: . . . I have loved you with an everlasting love, therefore I have continued my faithfulness to you. Again I will build you, and you shall be built, O *virgin* Israel" (Jer. 31:2–4; cf. also 2 Kings 19:21; Isa. 37:22; Jer. 31:21; Lam. 2:13). Luke's understanding of Mary's virginity was in line with this strong prophetic tradition; both narrator and readers understood the story as a fulfillment of God's promises to this virgin daughter Zion.

Similarly, a Christian prophet used the image of virginity to refer to the entire community of those who had been redeemed "from the *earth.*" They had been rescued from the deceitful signs of the earth beast and therefore could sing a new song, like Mary's, before the throne. John carefully identified those who were qualified to join in this choir. He called them virgins and then used other metaphors as synonyms of virginity (Rev. 14:1–5). These virgins are blameless, totally free of lying and deceit (those fingerprints of the devil). They "follow the Lamb wherever he goes" (presumably even to a cross). On their foreheads are written the names of the Lamb and his Father. They have been redeemed as firstfruit of the harvest, redeemed from humankind for God and the Lamb. They have won their battle with "the ancient serpent." The common denominator of all these metaphors is unconditional obedience to the First Commandment.

In this linguistic universe, such obedience defined virginity, and that definition applied to Luke's picture of Mary.

A similar pattern of thinking occurs in the *Epistle to Diognetus,* which defines salvation as sharing in the virginity of a trustworthy Eve: "Let your heart be knowledge and your life the true and comprehended word. And if you bear the tree of this and pluck its fruit, you will ever enjoy that which is desired by God, which the serpent does not touch, and deceit does not infect, and Eve is not corrupted, but a virgin is trusted, and salvation is set forth" (*Diognetus* 12.7–8).[5]

In this very way, the Lukan story assumes a perfect conjunction of wills between God and this descendant of Eve—her firstborn son would be God's firstborn as well. Mary's virginity reflected simultaneously God's gracious choice ("you have found favor with God") and her unqualified surrender ("here am I, a slave of the Lord"). That conjunction marked the transition from the old age to the new, justifying the sending of armies of angels to celebrate a divine plan that antedated both ages, an insight noted in this anonymous poem from the fifteenth century:

> Adam lay y-bunden
> Bunden in a bond
> Four thousand winter
> Thought he not too long.
>
> And all was for an apple,
> An Apple that he took,
> As clerkes finden
> Written in their book.
>
> Ne had the apple taken been,
> The apple taken been,
> Ne had never our Lady
> A been heavene queen.
>
> Blessed be the time
> That apple taken was,
> Therefore we moun singen
> Deo gracias.[6]

In the rest of the Gospel Luke never again refers to Gabriel's visit or to the virgin birth of Jesus. This fact suggests that Luke's concern was focused on God's salvation through the sending of his Son. It seems that Luke applied to Mary a reasoning similar to Paul's references to Adam: Just as Eve's sin had tempted Adam to sin and thus induced God's condemnation, so Mary's obedience opened the way for

Jesus' obedience, which brought about God's release of sinners from that condemnation. Luke used the story of Mary's "humiliation" to introduce the story of Jesus' "humiliation," and that story introduced, in turn, the year of the Lord's favor, with its gracious release of captives. Through his opening chapters, Luke assured Theophilus and other readers that the end of the story would confirm the good news from the Most High that angels had brought first to Zechariah, then to Mary, and finally to the shepherds.

If one looks around for a conclusion to these first two stories and a preface to the third, one could hardly improve on the poem of John Byrom:

> Let us, like these good shepherds then, employ
> Our grateful voices to proclaim the joy;
> Like Mary, let us ponder in our mind
> God's wondrous love in saving lost mankind.
> Artless and watchful, as these favoured swains,
> While virgin meekness in the heart remains,
> Trace we the Babe, who has retrieved our loss,
> From his poor manger to his bitter Cross;
> Treading his steps, assisted by his grace,
> Till man's first heavenly state again takes place.
> Then may we hope, the angelic thrones among,
> To sing, redeemed, a glad triumphal song.[7]

Notes

1. Søren Kierkegaard, *Philosophical Fragments,* trans. D. F. Swenson (Princeton, N.J.: Princeton University Press, 1942), 46.

2. Annie Dillard, "The Gospel According to Saint Luke," in *Incarnation,* ed. A. Corn (New York: Viking, 1990), 25. Used by permission of the author.

3. Johann Rist (1607–1667) in *Pilgrim Hymnal* (Boston: Pilgrim, 1962), 118. The uniqueness of this image of peace I have examined in "The Peace of God: Conceptions of Peace in the New Testament," *Celebrating Peace,* ed. L. S. Rouner (Notre Dame, Ind.: University of Notre Dame Press, 1990), 118–31.

4. John Milton, *Paradise Lost* (New York: New American Library, 1961), 5.385–90.

5. Translation by Kirsopp Lake, *The Apostolic Fathers,* Loeb Classical Library, 2 vols. (Cambridge, Mass.: Harvard University Press, 1912–13), II, 379.

6. Anonymous, *The New Oxford Book of Christian Poetry,* ed. D. Davie (Oxford: Oxford University Press, 1988), 21.

7. John Byrom, *New Oxford Book of Christian Poetry,* 155.

2

Jesus and Satan

The Sealing of the Covenant in Luke

His Death is the atonement for his death! . . .
His Death is the atonement for the whole race.[1]

The opening segments of the Gospel of Luke constitute a closely woven tapestry of prophecies and songs linked together by a continuing thread of narrative. That tapestry leads one to expect to find in later chapters much more intertextual linkage to Genesis than is usually found. Such linkage may appear after I sketch the infrastructure of assumptions and convictions that undergird what one may call the narrative theology of this Christian author. It is true that for him the story was the thing; one should therefore not try to dissolve the story into an abstract system of doctrine. But within and beneath the narrative one may discern an interlocking pattern of attitudes without which the story itself would break into a jumble of disconnected and isolated bits and pieces. Such a jumble is what most readers recall when they think of the many various episodes and teachings to be found in Luke-Acts.

Basic to everything were memories of the Genesis story of creation that traced all beginnings to God's Word *(logos)*, God's Spirit *(pneuma)*, God's Power *(dynamis)*. God's first act was to separate light from darkness. Everything that he created subsequent to that first action was good. This goodness embraced the earth itself, including every plant and animal on it. Together the earth and sea brought forth "every living creature that moves." The narrative made a special point of declaring the goodness of "wild animals [*thēria*, LXX] of the earth of every kind" and "everything that creeps on the ground" (Gen. 1:25). God finally created male and female "in our image, according to our likeness" (1:26). God gave them dominion over the wild animals and over the creeping things. God blessed them and gave them "every green plant for food" (1:30). Every good thing that

31

they might need was provided—under only one condition—that they refrain from eating the fruit of one tree. Even with this stipulation, everything remained very good (1:31). Each of these features in the story of creation may be found, either implicitly or explicitly, in Luke-Acts.

Equally basic to the infrastructure was the recollection of rebellion in Eden, with the resulting curses on the first creation. Genesis traced the instigation of rebellion to the serpent, "more crafty than any other wild animal" (*thērion*, 3:1, LXX). His craftiness succeeded in beguiling the woman, who, seeing how desirable was the forbidden fruit, accepted the serpent's assurance that she would not die if she ate it. She, in turn, persuaded her husband. Immediately on eating, they became aware of their nakedness before God. The results: a series of curses in which God decreed penalties for all who had shared in the corruption of his good creation—on the serpent and its seed; on the woman and her seed; on both husband and wife; on the earth, which would now frustrate the farmer's efforts; and on Cain, whose murder of Abel transmitted his parents' curse to his successors.

The character of the rebellion and the logic of the human situation following this series of divine condemnations insured that the succession of curses would continue to destroy the goodness of God's creation until God intervened to restore the *status quo ante*. Such an intervention required a new beginning in which God's Word, Spirit, and Power would again separate the darkness from the light. It required a "second Eve," a "slave of the Lord," a virgin free from the sin and the curse of Eve, and a recipient of God's pristine blessing. Moreover, this Eve must bear a son, conceived by the Spirit of God as the son of God, who would share God's blessing. He would be destined to rule over the house of Jacob forever. God would levy ominous demands on this son "born of a woman" (cf. Gal. 4:4–5). He must accept existence under the curse of enmity with the offspring of the serpent: "He [Eve's offspring] will strike your [the serpent's] head, and you will strike his heel" (Gen. 3:15). As an enemy, the serpent must be allowed to use maximum guile and power, a power that included the ultimate power to kill. As an enemy of the serpent, this son of woman must be able to strike the serpent's head, winning a final victory over the serpent's power to deceive, to tempt, to accuse, to threaten human beings with death. The son must win this victory by relying wholly on the Word, Spirit, and Power of God. As son of Adam and son of God, he must accept the curse on Adam (a return to the earth and exclusion from Eden) in order to win a victory over death and thus open the road for a return to paradise.

In chapter 1 I have uncovered the presence of these assumptions and convictions in the sequence of songs (the Benedictus, the Magnificat, the Doxology, the Nunc Dimittis), in the messages of Gabriel and the other angels, and in the revelations to both male and female prophets. I now explore the story of Jesus to see how the two remaining curses were lifted.

First I must examine a curse that remained in force throughout the following story—the promise of enmity between the offspring of the woman and the offspring of the serpent (Gen. 3:15). According to Gabriel's word, the blessing of Mary had freed her from that curse; but no such freedom was granted to her son. According to Mary's prophetic song, God would show strength with his arm, lifting up the humble and demoting the proud, enriching the poor and despoiling the rich, and thus fulfill the promises made to Abraham and his descendants. Such fulfillments, however, required that Mary's son win the long warfare with "the ancient serpent." Susan Garrett has shown that in dealing with Luke-Acts "one may scarcely over-estimate Satan's importance in the history of salvation. . . . It is Satan's fierce opposition to the purposes of God that renders Jesus' battle to effect salvation so necessary and so arduous, and his victory so great."[2] One may observe evidence for such an estimate in the care with which Luke introduces the first major battle between these two born enemies. The narrative of Jesus' baptism provided an important prelude to that battle. Jesus had accepted the good news as announced by John. While he was being baptized and was praying, the heavens were opened (a symbolic preparation for a prophetic vocation) and the Holy Spirit descended on him. This intervention was both a continuation of the Spirit's role in Jesus' birth and an authorization of his coming work as a prophet. First, it was a reminder of the presence of the Spirit in creation. Then came the voice of a Father acknowledging Jesus as his Son, beloved and blessed. In him John's prophecy would be fulfilled: "all flesh shall see the salvation of God" (Luke 3:6). This episode as a whole—proclamation, baptism, prayer, opening of heaven, descent of the Spirit, the word of God identifying his Son—Luke used all this to indicate how Jesus had been prepared for the opening battle with Satan, on the outcome of which the salvation of all flesh depended.

Next in the Lukan narrative, however, is a most surprising interruption, a genealogy that begins with Joseph and ultimately links Jesus to Adam, "the son of God." Not only is this an interruption for the readers of Luke; it is an unexplained alteration in the order of events in the Gospel of Mark, which Luke usually followed. In Mark, the story had moved from John's prediction of a successor who would baptize with the Holy Spirit, to Jesus' baptism, and then without a break to the forty days' trial in the wilderness (Mark 1:7–15). In this order of events, the testing of Jesus followed the baptism at once. Why did Luke insert the genealogy between those two strategic events?

I think the answer lies in his wish to provide a desirable background for the opening battle with the enemy. The baptismal recognition of Jesus as God's Son prepared the way for Satan's deceptive appeal, "if you are the Son of God. . . ." But the genealogy also prepared the way by recognizing Jesus' full vulnerability as son of Adam to Satan's stratagems. The genealogy (the usual order was reversed so that it would end in Adam) indicated that both the first Adam and Jesus were sons of God. Subtly it called on readers to compare and contrast Jesus' response to trial with the earlier responses of Eve, Adam, and Cain. There is an implicit contrast to Cain and an implicit likeness to firstborn Abel, the other son of Adam and the first shepherd. Accordingly, when the Spirit led Jesus into the wilderness, he was tested as all the descendants of Eve are tested. This testing was necessary if Jesus' victory were to make it possible for "all flesh" to receive God's timely power. Only thus could Jesus fulfill his baptismal vocation in which the Spirit empowered him to carry on such warfare as the Son of God.

Before looking in detail at that first battle, I should present evidence that in Luke's mind the Satan whom Jesus met in the wilderness was none other than the serpent who had lied to Eve in the garden. One may find such an identification in various late Jewish writings and in other early Christian writings (most clearly perhaps in Rev. 12:9). It should also be obvious that the functions of Satan in Luke 4 were the same as the functions of the serpent in Genesis 3: to use lies to deceive, then to use the deception to incite rebellion against God, and in this way to divert the human story away from God's creative designs. But more explicit evidence comes later in the Gospel: Jesus attributed his disciples' success in casting out demons to their ability to tread on serpents; moreover, Jesus linked this authority over *serpents* to the fall of *Satan* from heaven (Luke 10:17–19). In the same passage Satan is identified as "the enemy," an echo of Genesis 3:15. In Genesis this enemy had enough authority to triumph in the "time of trial"; in the Gospel the victory went to the son of Adam who was also the Son of God.

In the wilderness Satan used three deceptions in his efforts to test Jesus; all three failed. In two of his efforts Satan appealed to the words that God had used in Jesus' baptism by the Holy Spirit: "If you are the Son of God. . . ." That appeal reflected the universal human conception of what sonship to God should mean. The devil argued that to be a son of God was to inherit special privilege and to count on special immunities. By his better understanding of what sonship meant, Jesus proved to be invulnerable to such deception. By relying on the opposite logic Jesus was able to puncture the lie. Sonship to God did not exempt him from the conditions assigned to all children of Adam but required him to accept those conditions. The devil's appeal also reflected a basic misunderstanding of what God's fatherhood meant and therefore of the very nature of God's authority and power.

The second of the devil's tricks was a variant on the serpent's line in Genesis: "You will be like God." In this case Jesus would become like God in receiving the glory and power of all the kingdoms of the earth, a misconception again of fatherhood and sonship that finds almost universal acceptance. Jesus punctured this deception by his willingness as a human being to worship and serve God alone (the First Commandment). Such worship would be negated by any use of sonship for self-advancement, a conviction that was the opposite of Eve's.

In the third deception, the devil appealed to the multiple assurances in Psalm 91 of divine protection for those who trust in God: "No evil shall befall you" (v. 10). He thus turned truth into a lie. Jesus, however, recognized the deception: to utilize the truth for self-interest would be to "put the Lord your God to the test" (Luke 4:12). Thus, to defeat the deceiver he in effect fulfilled the divine promise that immediately followed the verse that the devil had quoted: "You will tread on the lion and the adder, the young lion and *the serpent* you will trample under foot" (Ps. 91:13). In such trampling, the psalmist almost certainly referred to God's initial curse on the serpent: "He will strike your head" (Gen. 3:15). By rejecting a false use of the truth, Jesus signaled the fulfillment of the archetypal curse.

One needs to explain why Luke placed this temptation last, when Matthew had placed it second. Why did Luke consider this to be the maximum test of Jesus' qualifications for his messianic work? Did he want to locate this trial at the most sacred place, the temple, thus anticipating the criminal trial that would soon be held there? Or did he want to suggest the similarity and contrast between this testing of Jesus and the prototypical testing of Eve, with the serpent's comforting assurance, "You will not die"? Did he want his readers to realize that an essential qualification for Jesus' successful ministry had been the acceptance, even before that ministry had begun, of the necessity of his death? Because this narrator knew that Jesus' final victory would be a victory over the fear of death, did he want to show at the outset that such a fear had already been mastered? Whatever may have been Luke's conscious intention, his account of Jesus' final trial pictured his enemies using the same basic appeal that Satan had used when they called on this king to authenticate his kingship by saving his own life (Luke 23:35–39). At the end as at the beginning, Satan's appeal was based on a false understanding of Jesus' sonship and therefore of God's fatherhood. It was that false understanding that Luke knew to be virtually universal in human thinking.

A modern idiom in legal and political circles may clarify the issues in Luke's account of the initial testing of Jesus: the idiom of a conflict of interest. In Genesis 3 Eve had a conflict between obeying God on the one hand and on the other a desire for food, for wisdom, and for beauty that could be gained only by claiming independence from God's authority. In Jesus' case, the conflict was again between obeying his Father at the cost of his life and a starving person's hunger, a powerless person's dreams of power, and a mortal's desire for freedom from dying. There is a strong resonance between the stories in Genesis 3 and Luke 4.

The wilderness trial was followed almost at once by the keynote sermon in Nazareth. The sermon began immediately with a quotation from Isaiah 61 that advanced the claim that Jesus had been commissioned by the Holy Spirit. Various signs of this authorization were itemized, such as good news for the poor and release to the captives. The sermon concluded with the amazing declaration of the fulfillment of the promise that the year of the Lord's favor had begun. Such a manifesto was surely designed to signal nothing less than the inception of a new age. In some respects these were signs of a new exodus, following patterns provided in the book of Deuteronomy. But the text in Isaiah 61 was also preceded by a chapter in which the features of a new *creation* were spelled out: the shining of an everlasting light, the end of violence and destruction, the gift of peace and righteousness. Just as the wilderness battle described a *before* that was essential to understanding Jesus' victories in the ensuing struggles with Satan, so the Nazareth manifesto described a *before* essential for understanding the liberating impact of those struggles. Both the wilderness trial and the synagogue manifesto marked the reversal of the success that the devil had achieved with the residents of Eden.

The first listener to penetrate the identity of this Son of God was an unclean demon: "I know who you are, the Holy One of God" (Luke 4:34). Because he knew who Jesus was, this descendant of the serpent recognized Jesus' superior power: "Have you come to destroy us?" Jesus answered that question: "Shut up and come out of him!" Luke described a typical day in Jesus' life in these terms: "Demons also came out of many, shouting, 'You are the Son of God'" (4:41). As victor over Satan, Jesus could destroy the hold that the demons had over their human hostages, though as yet only the demons knew the source of his authority.

In the Genesis saga, the power of the serpent had been demonstrated in the rebellion of Eve and Adam against the authority of God; in the Lukan antithesis, the power of the serpent and his descendants was destroyed by God's mercy in the forgiveness of sins. Accordingly, in the account of one of Jesus' first cures, the healing of a paralyzed man was attributed to Jesus' authority *on earth* to forgive sins (readers should recall the Genesis curses on the earth). Luke made it clear that both the healing of sickness and the forgiveness of sins were grounded in Jesus' mastery over the demons (5:17–26). Thus the year of the Lord's favor was initiated by a series of clearcut victories in the warfare between this offspring of Eve and the offspring of the serpent. Even a woman whom Satan had bound for eighteen years could be liberated (13:16)!

It was not long before Jesus "called the twelve together and gave them power and authority over all demons" (9:1). In fact, their proclamation of the kingdom was made the counterpart of the operation of this power. Jesus confirmed this linkage when he announced, "If it is by the finger of God that I cast out the demons, then the kingdom of God has come to you" (11:20).

On some occasions the disciples failed in exorcising an evil spirit. In that case Jesus condemned them as "a faithless and perverse generation" (9:41). But on their return from a successful foray into enemy territory, they said, "In your name even the demons submit to us" (10:17). Jesus' reply indicated that he had first held the authority he had given them and that this authority was superior to the power of "the enemy" (10:19). If they had felt any doubt that Jesus referred here to the primeval enemy, he removed it by declaring that in seeing these things his emissaries were seeing what prophets and kings had long hoped to see. His adversaries, however, could not see them, but were confident that "he casts out demons by Beelzebul, the ruler of the demons" (11:15).

In this connection one should note how often Jesus charged his enemies with being "an evil generation." A casual reading of this expression misses its original genetic, not temporal, thrust. What was in view was the kinship, the paternity, of these adversaries: they were children of the evil one. That is why they would join the residents of Tyre and Sidon, of Sodom and Gomorrah, in receiving God's judgment. Their birth united them with all those who had rejected the sign of Jonah or who had not, like the Egyptian queen, recognized the wisdom of Solomon. Their hostility to the prophets stamped them with the mark of Cain (11:42–52). Each age, old and new, had its own children, its own generative power (16:8). One's generation was a matter of choice, not of birthday; that choice determined paternity. The point is important and one should not dismiss it hastily. In early Christian parlance, God has many children but no grandchildren. The same is true of God's adversary, the serpent, with his various aliases. The heirs of Adam and Eve may belong to different generations, but not so the children of God or of the devil. The Lukan stories depict the emerging conflict between these two families and the final resolution of that conflict when the victory of Jesus became the grounds for "good news of great joy."

Notice how Luke recounted the lifting of another curse on Adam and on Cain; that curse had been spelled out in some detail:

> Cursed is the earth where you work;
>> in toil you will eat of it all the days of your life;
> thorns and thistles it will bring forth for you,
>> and you will eat the grass of the field.
> By the sweat of your face
>> you will eat your bread
> until you return to the earth,
>> for out of it you were taken;
> you are earth,
>> and to the earth you will return.
>> (Gen. 3:17–19, LXX, my trans.)

In this verdict one should note first the emphasis on the alienation of mortals from the earth as their intended home, the good earth of Genesis 1 that had become the sterile and unfriendly earth of Genesis 3. Luke was well aware of this feature in God's curse and recounted various episodes that illustrated both the alienation and its resolution. For example, when Jesus first summoned fishermen to follow him, they who had found no success in the night's trawling found in the dawn, when they obeyed Jesus' instructions, their nets filled to the breaking point, two boats full. Human dominion "over the fish of the sea" had been restored (Gen. 1:26). (A variant of the same story in John 21:1–8 links the catch of fish to the disciples' obedience to the command of the *risen* Jesus, a symbol of his authority, of their mission, and of the restored dominion over God's creation.) One may also detect echoes of this restored dominion in the account of the disciples' ability in the wilderness to feed five thousand people when they obeyed this provider. The bread given from heaven and blessed

by the Messiah was an implicit reminder of Adam's difficulties in se-
curing bread *(artos)* from the earth. So, too, the grass *(chortos)* on
which, in the other Gospels, the crowds were commanded to recline,
may have recalled Adam's penalty—in hunger to be forced to eat the
grass *(chortos)* of the field (Mark 6:39; Gen. 3:18, LXX).

Throughout Luke the picture of Jesus is of one who conveyed to
faithful followers a freedom from anxiety for food and clothing. Like
the birds and flowers, they had come under the primal blessing and
care of their heavenly Father. When Jesus sent his delegates into the
various towns of Galilee without purse or bag or extra provisions, they
received lodging and food in response to their gift of peace. So, too,
their Master, who had no place to lay his head, did not lack for hos-
pitality; indeed it was so abundant that he was accused of being "a
glutton and a drunkard." When, on crossing the lake, his companions
became panic-stricken with danger from the gale-driven waves, he
had power to calm the storm and to rebuke them for their fears, another sign of the goodness of this sea and of the restoration of human
dominion over it (Gen. 1:21, 28). All this was evidence in narrative
form of the end of the hostility between the earth and sea and the descendants of Adam. The various stories thus pointed to the truth that
was hidden in them. The prophecies of Isaiah, themselves resonant
with the creation epic, were being fulfilled: mountain peaks were
being leveled, ravines filled in, paths straightened as signs of the year
of the Lord's favor.

In the same creation epic, the final condemnation of Adam and Eve
had been their separation from the tree of life. Luke treated that aspect of the story as far more than an etiological curiosity, that is, a myth
to explain the origin of human mortality. To him this story defined
death as due to a broken covenant with God that automatically excluded God's human "image" from the tree of life. Such mortality
could be overcome only by a new action of forgiveness when God read-
mitted the guilty to his good earth. The serpent's lie, "You will not die,"
had provoked their eviction from paradise. That victory of the serpent
could be reversed only when a son of Adam, by dying, defeated the deception of the devil and reopened access to the tree of life.

In my judgment, this point touches on the basic reason that Luke,
even more than the other Gospels, stressed the necessity for the Messiah's death: "The Son of Man must undergo great suffering, and be
rejected by the elders, chief priests, and scribes [those guilty of the
blood of Abel, 11:50], and be killed, and on the third day be raised"
(9:21–22). Already in his opening chapters, Luke had probably recognized this necessity (2:34–35): it had been implied in the trial of

Jesus in the wilderness; it was symbolized in the effort to kill Jesus after his opening manifesto in the Nazareth synagogue. But the necessity of mortal suffering is hidden from his enemies, who in their blindness "do not know what they are doing" (23:34). It had been hidden even from his closest followers, of whom Luke wrote: "they did not understand this saying; its meaning was concealed from them" (9:45; see 18:34). Jesus had been prepared for his own final time of trial, but they had not been ready for theirs (22:40–46). In part, their lack of readiness had been due to the unconditional character of his demands that all who followed him must share his rejection and crucifixion. In part, it was due to Satan's success in deceiving them (more about this point in a later passage; see p. 43).

Luke's vocabulary could depict the victory over death in various images. For example, in Paul's final official trial before King Agrippa he described the changes produced by Jesus with several expressions:

an opening of the eyes of the blind,

a turning from darkness to light,

an acceptance of the forgiveness of sins,

a place among those made holy by their faith in Jesus,

a call to witness to visions of the risen Lord.

All of these in Luke's vocabulary represented a turning "from the power of Satan to God"; in other words, all constituted an authentic victory over the primeval curse (Acts 26:17–18).

But now I should deal more directly with the basic curse of death and with its removal through the fulfillment of the requirement that "the Son of Man must die." One could say that all this was necessary simply because it happened that way, and all explanations are produced after the fact. Although it might satisfy a modern mentality, such an answer does not do justice to the biblical mentality. Many questions remain. Why was it necessary for Jesus to be betrayed into the hands of his enemies? Why did this necessity include so terrible a role for the chief priests? How was the rising from the dead linked to the necessity for this suffering? Luke was well aware of these profound mysteries, which he required his readers to ponder.

Chapter 24 furnishes some clues to his understanding of the puzzle. Here one finds an intimate discussion between Jesus and his disciples about the problems posed by his death. The most clarifying conversation takes place between Jesus and two disciples on the road to Emmaus, the longest of the visits with the risen Lord (Luke

24:13–32). These two disciples had not been previously mentioned in Luke: Cleopas and an unnamed companion, whom an early mosaic identified with Luke himself. The central purpose for this appearance of Jesus was to explain why his death had been necessary. The explanation required an opening of the scriptures, and it was this opening that occasioned a "burning" within their hearts (24:32). Before that discussion the disciples had wondered if the crucifixion of this prophet had destroyed their hope that he would be the one to redeem Israel. After the conversation, that hope came alive again. In the eyes of their unknown interlocutor, their assumption that the death of Jesus had been the end showed them to be fools. Their hearts had been too hardened to believe "all that the prophets have declared" (24:25). "'Was it not necessary that the Messiah should suffer these things and then enter into his glory?' Then beginning with Moses and all the prophets, he interpreted to them the things about himself in all the scriptures" (24:26–27).

One must concede that there were ample reasons for foolishness. The scribes, whose knowledge of the scriptures was extensive, were unaware of such prophecies. Even today, scholars find it difficult to locate the specific texts that Jesus had in mind. One must also observe that in Luke's story the bewilderment was dispelled not so much by specific texts or by verbal explanations as by the moment at supper when "he took bread, blessed and broke it, and gave it to them" (24:30–31, a reminder of the covenant in his blood, 22:20).

After they had returned to Jerusalem and rejoined the other disciples, Jesus undertook again to explain why his passion had been essential to his vocation: "These are my words that I spoke to you while I was still with you—that everything written about me in the law of Moses, the prophets, and the psalms must be fulfilled . . . that the Messiah is to suffer and to rise from the dead on the third day, and that repentance and forgiveness of sins is to be proclaimed in his name to all nations, beginning from Jerusalem" (24:44–47).

Here and elsewhere in the Gospel the point was made that such suffering was needed before repentance and forgiveness could be proclaimed in Jesus' name. This point suggests a line of thought that has received too little attention. Many prophets had relayed God's promises to Israel, promises of healing and redemption, of life and joy, of the restoration of justice and triumph over all enemies. Luke traced the frustration of these promises to the fratricidal conflict between Cain and Abel, and before that, by implication, to God's curses on the serpent, the earth, Adam and Eve, and all of their progeny. If God's promises were to be fulfilled, the first book of Moses had made clear what was necessary: nothing less than the removal of these initial curses through the intervention of God's grace and favor. The curse of death must be overcome by life; only then could repentance and forgiveness of sins be proclaimed to all of Adam's children. That last statement of Jesus to his followers (Luke 24:46–47) made the linkage clear: it was his act of suffering that made their repentance possible. The same act conveyed forgiveness from God for all rebellions against God. The demonstration of God's love for all God's enemies in the dying of the Son for them fulfilled the requirements whereby a new age could succeed the old.

In his version of the passion story Luke told how the powers of this new age began to operate among three separate groups: the Gentiles, of whom the penitent criminal was representative; the leaders of Israel, whom Jesus had accused of guilt for the blood of all the prophets since the murder of Abel; and, finally, the disciples, who had betrayed the covenant that had been sealed with them in the blood of Jesus.

Taking these three in reverse order, I first examine the ways in which the death of Jesus was necessary in gaining the repentance and forgiveness of those who had sworn to follow him. One may best see how Jesus countered their foolishness and hardness of heart in the discussion around the table in the upper room, immediately preceding the arrest. In this discussion Luke cited extensively Isaiah 53: "he *poured* out himself to death" (Isa. 53:12); that action was strongly echoed in Jesus' words, "This cup that is *poured out* for you is the new covenant in my blood" (Luke 22:20). Soon after those words were spoken, a conflict broke out as to which disciple was greatest, a horrible and savage irony. Jesus tried to counter their rivalries for superiority with his declaration, "I am among you as one who serves." That form of servanthood could refer only to the pouring out of his blood for them.

Luke then cited another line from Isaiah: "For I tell you, this scripture must be fulfilled in me: 'And he was counted among the lawless'" (Luke 22:37; Isa. 53:12, LXX). Who were these lawless? It is not strange that later Christian interpreters should think of the two criminals, but the context makes it clear that Luke meant it to refer to those same disciples. They had broken his earlier command to do their work without purse or bag; now they produced both—clear signs not only of outright disobedience but of a fatal misunderstanding of his mission. Indeed, when they confessed to carrying two swords he declared the fulfillment of scripture: "what is written about me is being fulfilled" (Luke 22:37).

In what way did Luke think of them as transgressors? The right answer has often been overlooked because of later debates about pacifism and the legitimacy of using force in self-defense. Such a general ethical issue was far from Luke's intention. To him, these disciples were transgressors not only because they were enslaved to forbidden standards of superiority (vv. 24–27) but even more because they were not ready to join him in "the new covenant in my blood." That is, they were far from ready to die with him for their enemies. It was they who were fulfilling this scripture!

Evidence that this was Luke's concern is provided by his use of another line from Isaiah's prophecy: "he bore the sin of many and made intercession for the transgressors" (Isa 53:12; Luke 22:32, 37). For whom was that intercession made at the table when he sealed the new covenant with them? The answer cannot be mistaken: Peter and his companions. "Simon, Simon, listen! Satan has demanded to sift *all* of you like wheat" (Luke 22:31). Satan was trying to sift or deceive them. After Jesus' death, Satan's enmity would shift from Jesus to his messengers. That was why it was necessary for him to make intercession for them: "I have *prayed for you* that your own faith may not fail; and you, when once you have turned back, strengthen your brothers" (22:32).

In his response Simon proved himself to be the first "transgressor" who needed Jesus' "intercession." Satan had already deceived him, so that he thought he was ready to go with Jesus "to prison and to death" (22:33). If ever there was a successful lie on Satan's part this was it. As long as Simon and his companions misunderstood the covenant "in my blood," they were not yet fully qualified to "eat and drink at my table in my kingdom" (v. 30). Thus Jesus' intercession for these transgressors provided the necessary prelude, the essential *before,* to their later drinking from his cup. For Luke, these very transgressors were included in the fulfillment of Isaiah's promises of forgiveness: "The righteous one, my servant, shall make many righteous, and he shall bear *their* iniquities" (Isa. 53:11).

The second group for whom Jesus' death was necessary consisted of those who ever since the Nazareth proclamation had tried to kill this messianic claimant. When the risen Messiah commanded his delegates to begin their work "from Jerusalem," he had in mind the very people who had been responsible for his death. One may draw some inferences from Jesus' identification of these opponents as guilty of the blood of all the prophets since Cain had killed Abel (Luke 11:50–51). One inference is that Jesus and his messengers could be identified with Abel. Another is that the crucifixion of Jesus could be

interpreted as the Genesis tragedy updated, one brother killing another over the acceptability of their two sacrifices by God. Part of the
irony of this updating is that when Jesus' enemies demanded his execution, they also demanded the release of a *murderer*, like them a descendant of Cain (23:18–25)!

But unlike the blood of Abel, the blood of Jesus was the seal of a
new covenant between God and his people since it was blood poured
out for God's very enemies as an expression of God's love for them,
as illustrated by the prayer that Jesus uttered from the cross: "Father,
forgive them; for they do not know what they are doing" (23:34). This
verse may not have been in the original edition of the Gospel; perhaps some early editor inserted it as entirely consistent with the action as a whole, as both a call to repentance and an assurance of
forgiveness. This editor would not have included the prayer apart
from confidence that the Father had answered it. That fact entitles
one to examine it more closely.

Who were to be forgiven? Surely "the chief priests, the leaders, and
the people" (23:13). For what were they to be forgiven? For their
share in the bloodguiltiness of Cain? For their handing the Messiah
over to the Gentiles? For the preference they gave to Barabbas? For
their efforts to defend their own status and prestige against Jesus' at-
tacks? For their attribution of Jesus' power to Beelzebul? For their
role as false shepherds of God's people, claiming to know the God
whom they did not know? For their rejection of God's forgiveness and
grace, blind to the possibility of a new creation? Perhaps for all these
reasons. One basis for the appeal was "they do not know what they are
doing." Again, narrative theology invites many answers to the question, What didn't they know? though it rules out final certainty about
any of the answers. They did not know that they were joining Cain in
their action. They did not know that they were putting God's Son to
death. They did not know that through his death God was lifting the
curses that had been in force since the expulsion from Eden. They
did not know that the unanticipated result of their success would be
God's victory over Satan and over death, a victory that would trigger
"good news of great joy for all the people"—*beginning from Jerusalem.*
This prayer forever rules out any resentment or hatred against the so-
called Christ killers; it forever destroys the use of violence against any
so-called enemies of God or of Christ; it forever excludes any Christian who indulges in such hostility from sharing "the new covenant in
my blood." In its wide range of implications, the prayer in itself con-
stitutes a major sign of the reversal of the Genesis curses on all successors to Cain.

Present on the stage for Luke's Oberammergau was a third group: Gentiles who were neither enemies nor disciples, individuals who were there through no choice of their own, though they had other sins on their slates. For them, too, Jesus' death opened a way into the Garden of Eden, past the flaming sword that barred the way to the tree of life. Luke gives a vignette of enacted forgiveness in the last moments before Jesus expired. He reported this conversation between Jesus and one of the criminals crucified with him:

THE CRIMINAL: "Jesus, remember me when you come into your kingdom."

JESUS: "Truly I tell you, today you will be with me in Paradise."
                                                    (23:42–43)

In this reply, the first word "truly" (amēn), pointed to the following announcement as an authoritative disclosure of God's will; Jesus was speaking ex cathedra from the cross as his throne. This reply was in sharp contrast to the request, for Jesus replaced the vague "when" of the petitioner with the sharp definiteness of "today." Luke understood the day of Jesus' death as marking a total transformation in the human situation. Now repentance and forgiveness could begin.

Jesus' promise "you will be with me" provokes several inferences. Even before the risen Lord had commissioned his disciples, the repentance of this nondisciple had established a solidarity with Jesus that was still closed to them. The unnamed criminal's recognition of his own guilt, his acceptance of punishment, his testimony to Jesus' innocence—these had established a solidarity that could not be broken by the death of either or both. In fact, by receiving God's forgiveness the criminal became the first witness to the presence of the kingdom. Jesus' reply turned thought away from a kingdom that might dawn sometime in the future to a return to paradise "today" (as in Rev. 2:7). On the one hand, this answer corrected views of the kingdom that were held by Jesus' opponents (vv. 37–38, 42), and, on the other hand, it explicitly announced that God had lifted the ban against any return to the garden. This supports the conclusion that, from the first chapters of his Gospel, Luke discerned in the death and resurrection of Jesus God's final removal of the curses on the children of Eve (the unremitting enmity of the serpent) and the curse on Adam (the alienation from the earth and a return to that earth). At the very moment when others were taunting Jesus with cries for him to save himself, the Messiah had saved one other person by refusing to save himself. The dying of the innocent son of Adam/Son of God had opened the way for all the children of Adam to return to the tree of life.

As Luke handled this anecdote, it became a fitting preparation for the final commissioning of Jesus' messengers to call *all nations* to repentance and forgiveness. The words of the felon became a universal confession of sins, just as the words of Jesus became a promise of universal amnesty to all other penitent descendants of Adam. This felon offered his own explanation of the necessity for the Messiah's suffering. Apart from the crucifixion of Jesus, he would never have seen paradise and would never have been able to disclose the terms on which others like him could share in the new creation.

I may now call attention to a final inference. Having been persuaded by this range of evidence that as Luke edited his version of the story of Jesus he had in mind the lifting of the primeval curses, one is more likely to find in the story of Mary's obedience the antithesis to the story of Eve's disobedience, and to find in the story of the shepherds a symbolic removal of God's curse on the earth. Conclusions of this sort would be nothing new in the long history of biblical exegesis, even though they have been relatively dormant in recent times. Of an earlier awareness of this intertextual skeleton of assumptions and attitudes, only one witness need be called here. He was a blind poet writing in prison, where he was being held as punishment for dissident political activity. Speaking of Jesus' crucifixion and addressing his own readers directly, John Milton interpreted Jesus' death as a fulfillment and a reversal of the curse in Genesis 3:15:

> This godlike act
> Annuls thy doom, the death thou shouldst have died,
> In sin forever lost from life; this act
> Shall bruise the head of Satan, crush his strength,
> Defeating Sin and Death, his two main arms.
> And fix far deeper in his head their stings
> Than temporal death shall bruise the Victor's heel,
> Or those whom He redeems.[3]

As an editor, Luke expressed a similar conviction when he told of the appearances of the risen Jesus to his disciples. He carefully dated those appearances "on the first day of the week," a phrase that resonates with the Genesis story of the first day. The specific phrase "at early dawn" reminded readers of God's first creative words, "Let there be light." Further, Luke crowded into that single day the entire series of meetings: the dawn rendezvous with the women; the evening meal with Cleopas and his companion en route to Emmaus; their return to Jerusalem and report to the other disciples; Jesus' visit with them and his gift of peace; finally, his withdrawal into heaven after his final instructions. That all these should have happened on the first day of the week was a telling symbol: the gift of light, life, the Spirit, power, the breaking of bread, a morning message and evening visit, the opening of eyes, and the promise of forgiveness—all belonged on the first day.

This series was not only a fitting climax to the Gospel but also a preparation for a second volume, well named the Acts of the Apostles. The Gospel presented in narrative form a series of decisive *befores* that were necessary if Theophilus and other Christian readers were to understand fully what had happened among them. In earlier sections of this essay I have examined the infrastructure of assumptions and convictions that one can discern within and behind the Gospel accounts of the shepherds, Mary, and Jesus. I have suggested the extent to which that infrastructure was influenced by the Genesis pictures of Creation and Fall. Now, in following the doings of the apostles, one finds an infrastructure that was shaped not only by the same scriptures but also by the preceding volume. The "acts" of the apostles fulfilled an extensive cluster of prophecies that had been articulated in Luke's first volume.

Those acts continued to mark the transition between the two ages, old and new, that had been accomplished by God through a return to the conditions prevailing between Creator and creation before the old age had been polluted. Luke's second volume introduced a roster of new characters, but the patterns of relationship between God and Satan, between old age and new, remained constant. The attention of both narrator and listeners remained focused on happenings in the imagined realms, where the eyes of prophets could penetrate to the place where the Word, the Spirit, and the Power of God were overcoming the lies and deceptions of Satan. Those potencies were now being mediated through the risen Messiah and through persons sent by him who exercised authority in his name. Their chief adversaries continued to live in the imagined world of the devil, with his puppet demons that sought to exercise authority through various human channels. The primary human actors had been introduced in the Gospel—the followers of Jesus, his opponents among the religious leaders, and the bystanders who had no direct involvement in the religious hostility but who became part of the audience addressed by the apostles.

In many episodes in the book of Acts this warfare emerged, as it had emerged in the Gospel, in the fulfillment of Jesus' assignment to cast out demons. In both volumes, this assignment was coordinated with the authorization to heal the sick and to forgive sins. Just as all these works of liberation were opposed by the ruler of the demons, so, too, they were accomplished in the name of Jesus, deeds deriving from his power, or even as done by his hand (Acts 4:28). Through his messengers, the risen Jesus continued to liberate captives of the devil, enabling them to return to their prelapsarian existence.

In the book of Acts as in the Gospel, an essential test of strength in this Messiah/serpent struggle was which one of them could wield ultimate power and authority over death (the ultimate curse in Genesis 3), through fear of which Satan had established his kingdom over the hearts of humankind. Because the primeval sin had prompted the curse of death, any victory over the devil must reach, as the hymnist Isaac Watts has written, "far as the curse is found"; that is, it must provide resources sufficient to overcome both sin and death. (The common linkage of these two terms, "sin" and "death," in early Christian thinking may itself be a silent reminder of Genesis 3.) The Messiah had fulfilled that requirement in the assignment he had received from his Father—to be crucified and to be raised from the dead. That victory made possible the proclamation of repentance and forgiveness of sin to all nations, beginning from Jerusalem. The apostles were sent out by the risen Master to announce that victory and to demonstrate its current power.

So much by way of an analysis of the infrastructure. Now I turn to the successive narratives themselves to see how Luke shaped them to disclose how God's design from the beginning had made possible this result: the shift from God's curse to God's blessing. I limit this phase of study to the opening chapters of Acts, believing that in them, as in the opening chapters of the Gospel, the narrator was able to provide a broad preview of all that was to follow.

In the first few verses of Acts, Luke binds the two volumes together by linking everything in the subsequent episode to the story of Jesus' final commission and to the gift of the Holy Spirit. Before being taken up into heaven, Jesus had given instructions through the Holy Spirit to "the apostles whom he had chosen" (Acts 1:2).

"The apostles whom he had chosen" are those with whom he had eaten in the upper room and on whom he had conferred a kingdom. He had promised them "thrones judging the twelve tribes of Israel" (Luke 22:29–30). He had earlier given them "power and authority over all demons" (9:1). Their ability "to tread on serpents" (10:19) had been an echo of Gen. 3:15 and therefore a hint of a return to the situation in Eden before Eve's deception by the serpent.

The "instructions through the Holy Spirit" recalled many things: the baptism and wilderness trial of Jesus, the predictions of John the Baptist, the conception of Jesus, the prophecies of Zechariah, all resonant with the work of the Spirit of God in the creation of all things. This Spirit had formed the primary link between the work of Jesus and the call of his disciples. At the end of the Gospel he had commanded them to wait in Jerusalem for "the promise of the Father": "You will be baptized with the Holy Spirit" (Acts 1:4–5). In the Gospel (Luke 24:49) this baptism had been made equivalent with being "clothed with power from on high." This conjunction of Word, Spirit, and Power had undergirded Luke's epic from the story of Mary to the end (Luke 1:26–38). The conjunction of the three formed a continuing link between the work of the twelve apostles on earth, the will of their Lord in heaven, and the Jesus who had promised to return (Acts 1:11). So the infrastructure of thought provided the skeleton not only of the narrative but also of the events themselves.

The first significant event was the replacement of Judas by Matthias, an episode motivated clearly by the desire to keep intact the number twelve as witnesses to the resurrection. Another motive on the part of the narrator was to carry forward the memory of Jesus' promise at the Last Supper regarding the need for their permanent role as "judges" of the tribes of Israel. The narrator had in mind not only their future governance but also their function as a return to the *status quo ante*, God's intention before the birth of the twelve patriarchs, the prophet-sons of Jacob-Israel.

The whole of Acts 2 consists of an account of what happened in Jerusalem at the Festival of Pentecost. The events constituted a dramatic fulfillment of the prophecies that had appeared not only in scripture but in the Gospel as well. They also constituted a dramatic prelude to the whole of Luke's second volume, in ways similar to the role of the Nazareth sermon in the first volume. Because the links to previous and succeeding events are numerous, and because the implications are far-reaching, I limit my comments to inferences that clearly reflect the underlying infrastructure of attitudes. I first cite significant phrases and then comment on the narrator's intention.

"They were all together in one place." Here the narrator underscores not only the relevance of this event to all followers of Jesus but its universal significance as well.

"All of them were filled with the Holy Spirit." These words establish continuity of thought with the opening of this volume, with the ending of the previous volume, with the baptism and testing of Jesus, with the announcement made by John the Baptist, with the conception of Jesus and the blessing of Mary, with the word of God in the Law, the Prophets, and the Psalms—back to the breath of God that had first summoned light out of darkness.

"All of them . . . began to speak in other languages, as the Spirit gave them ability. . . . Each one heard them speaking in the native language of each." The miracle of speaking induced a miracle of hearing; the result was a cancellation of God's curse on Babel (Gen. 11:1–9) and a return of human communication to the *status quo ante* Babel.

"Parthians, Medes . . . both Jews and proselytes." Included here are not only the physical descendants of Abraham but all the Gentiles who had been converted to Israel through the centuries. Thus the message reached the entire house of Israel, the entire lineage of Abraham, beginning in Jerusalem but including a far-flung Diaspora. The blessing leaped over limitations of space, time, and racial descent.

"We hear them speaking about God's deeds of power." Spirit-powered—all these terms pointed to God's presence within and behind what was happening. God was doing something new through the death and resurrection of Jesus.

"This is what was spoken through the prophet Joel." Spoken by whom? Through whom? A spokesman of God. Saying what? I will pour out *my* Spirit (Joel 2:28–32). Accomplishing what? Making all recipients prophets of the new day.

"Everyone who calls on the name of the Lord shall be saved." "Everyone" indicates the universality of God's intention because it allows no exception. That inclusiveness implies a return to the time before the separation of humanity into nations and religions.

"In the last days . . . the coming of the Lord's great and glorious day." The word assured not only a return to the beginnings but also a "fast forward" to final judgment and redemption. The gift of the Spirit marks the fulfillment of God's plan for all things.

"The sun shall be turned to darkness." This portent in Joel's prophecy was both eschatological and protological; the coming failure of sun and moon would open the way back to the first day of creation. Joel definitely had in mind the lifting of the curse on the earth levied in Genesis 3 (Joel 2:18–27).

"Jesus of Nazareth . . . you crucified and killed by the hands of those outside the law." This event was in accordance with the definite plan and foreknowledge of God. The necessity of death was recognized, a death that marked the power of Satan and the sin of humankind; but this necessity was grounded in God's plan before that sin, that is, before the events of Genesis 3.

"God raised him up, having freed him from death, because it was impossible for him to be held in its power. . . . He was not abandoned to Hades, nor did his flesh experience corruption." The death was real, but it represented not the power of death or Satan but victory over both death and Satan; it therefore canceled the curse of God on Adam and his descendants, the curse of earth returning to the earth.

"For David says concerning him, 'I saw the Lord always before me . . . therefore . . . my flesh will live in hope. . . .' The Lord said to my Lord, 'Sit at my right hand, until I make your enemies my footstool.'" God had placed Jesus at God's right hand until God had subjected all enemies to this king, ending the enmity promised in Genesis 3:15. The Lord antedated David, and his kingdom antedated David's kingdom.

"Peter said to them, 'Repent, and be baptized every one of you in the name of Jesus Christ, so that your sins may be forgiven; and you will receive the gift of the Holy Spirit. . . . Save yourselves from this corrupt generation.'" The alternatives were clear. On the one hand, to continue to live as members of a corrupt generation, composed of all the descendants of Eve and Adam, in unbroken solidarity with their sin and death; on the other hand, by repentance and forgiveness, to become the heirs of a new generation, freed from the entail of sin and death through the gift of God's Spirit.

"The promise is for you, for your children, and for all . . . whom the Lord our God calls to him." One cannot fail to notice the double message to Jerusalem: You, *you* who crucified and killed the Author of life. The promise is for *you* and for your *children*. It is the promise of forgiveness that would break the endless cycle of sin. Those who were called to him formed a community that Luke pictured in terms of freedom from the frustrations described in the Genesis curses on the earth. Thus the initial result of the work of the apostles confirmed the promises made in the Gospel.

The story of Pentecost raises a general question of some importance. What is the relation of the narrative as history to the narrative as theology? Here, as elsewhere, one should distinguish between a "true story" and a "truth story." As a historical narrative the story is not credible. Few readers are able to accept all details in the story as facts that objective observers could have verified: the numbers of people involved, the range of nations in view, the accuracy of the *all*s and the *every*s, the picture of the ensuing life of three thousand people. Did Luke try to tell a true story, a credible picture of events in the visible, public world? If he tried he failed. But he seems to have been more interested in truth of a different order within a different world of thought—the imagined world in which the primary reality was the activity of the Word, the Spirit, and Power of God. He was too sophisticated an author to expect that the historical narrative would be credible. He may rather have had a quite different aim as he recounted this incredible historical narrative: he may have wanted to stress the importance of the credibility of the narrative theology. He may have consciously used the impossibility at one level to call attention to the possibility at another level, the human impossibility that pointed beyond itself to the divine possibility, similar to the truth revealed by Gabriel (Luke 1:37). In any case, one cannot doubt that it was the narrative theology, the truth story, that was of primary concern to this editor; and readers should keep this point in mind when they react to other incredible features of the stories in Acts.

In the Gospel the Nazareth manifesto of Jesus was followed immediately by accounts of his mastery over demons. So in Acts the Pentecost manifesto of the apostles was followed by their cure of a forty-year-old man who had been lame from birth. The power to heal this man stemmed from the faith in the name of Jesus. The reaction among the rulers and elders (4:5) was the same as in the Gospel. On one side, the leaders of Israel; on the other, the God of Abraham, Isaac, and Jacob and of all the prophets since Samuel. These were the same adversaries that Jesus had charged with the blood of all the prophets since Abel. They had rejected "the *Author* of life" (3:15). The irony of this alignment was underscored by the contrast between their murder of this "Author" and their request for amnesty for Barabbas, a murderer (3:14). This contradiction was exceeded by another: the "Author of life" whom they had murdered had been directed by God to go first *to them* "to bless you, by turning each of you from your wicked ways" (3:25–26). This child of God had been able to wipe out the sin they had shared with Cain. Because Jesus had lifted God's curse on Cain, all that was needed for the renewal of life was their repentance (3:19–20). These murderers could participate in the "time of universal restoration" (3:20); forgiveness was available to them, because the apostles, like Jesus, recognized that these murderers did not know what they were doing (3:17). God had predestined all this to take place (4:28), a clear reference to a design that had been present with God even *before* the rebellions of Eve and her descendants. (Such priority was also implied in the title "the Author of life.") The words of Peter that had been prompted by the Holy Spirit had now been confirmed by the approval of the same Spirit (4:8, 31–37). This Spirit, in turn, had been released when God had won a victory over sin and death in the obedience of "the Author of life," the Messiah who had been murdered on orders from this very council.

After this confrontation with the council, the apostles reported to the entire company of believers (4:23ff.). The narrator paints an idyllic picture of this new paradise: "they were all filled with the Holy

Spirit." The word was spoken with boldness, songs were sung in exuberant joy, all had "one heart and soul." Not a person was in need, for no one claimed private wealth; all resources were held in common. In short, "great grace was upon them all" (4:33). In this context "great" is an eschatological adjective that suggests the finality and inclusiveness of divine forgiveness.

The narrator soon made clear, however, that baptism by the Spirit carried inescapable risks. It was as true of these messianists as it had been true of the Messiah that the gift of the Spirit provoked a new time of testing by the devil. Which would prove to be stronger, the serpent or the Spirit? Accordingly, chapter 5 presents Ananias and Sapphira, two descendants of Adam and Eve, on whom Satan used the same ploy—a lie that they accepted. With other baptized believers they had sold their property to add money to the common fund. Some of their profit they donated to the community, but the rest they retained. The apostle discerned what had happened in their hearts in the struggle between Satan and the Spirit. "Why has Satan filled your heart to lie to the Holy Spirit?" (5:3).

At this point Luke's readers would no doubt have recalled Peter's own defeat by Satan, as well as Jesus' victory during the forty-day trial. They would have seen in this last triumph of Satan a sign of the presence and power of the old age; in Peter's question they would have seen a sign of the presence and power of the new. In the old age an acceptance of Satan's deception meant death; even in the new, when believers who had received the Spirit lied to the Spirit, the sin made death automatic. One could make no compromise between new and old; any relapse from control by the Spirit to control by Satan signaled the death of the new self and exclusion from the new community. By his resurrection Jesus had been given the authority to exercise judgment over such betrayal through his disciples. Luke's historical narrative was shaped to express this truth of narrative theology. The incredibility of the sudden death of both sinners disclosed to Christian readers the credibility of their return to the realm of sin and death. What was axiomatic in narrative theology became automatic in the historical narrative.

Another instance of the conflict between the two ages was provided in the following story of the imprisonment of the apostles on orders of the high priest (5:17–42). The prison was securely locked, with guards standing at the doors so that captives could not have escaped through the doors. Yet the apostles were found in the temple "teaching the people." Hauled before their captors, the apostles succeeded in bringing "this man's blood on us" (cf. Luke 11:50). Yet in proclaiming guilt for having killed Jesus, these messengers from Jesus offered repentance and forgiveness of sins to the same representatives of Israel.

The narrative is replete with the symbolic language of the good news. Liberation took place at night; the call to repentance took place at daybreak. The prison, securely locked, was replaced by the open courts of the temple. Obedience to human authority yielded to obedience to God. The fears and jealousy of the captors accented the courage and selflessness of the apostles. The frustrated efforts of the council reminded readers of many earlier frustrations of the same order (Luke 4:28–30; 13:31–33; 19:47–48; 20:19, 26; 22:2). Prison meant no frustration for the disciples, who used the occasion to fulfill Jesus' command; their message followed word for word the instructions from the risen Lord (Luke 24:47–49; Acts 5:31–32). Again, the evangelist was demonstrating his adeptness in using historical narrative, in itself literally incredible, to stress the central accents in his narrative theology. Here the twelve were beginning their true work of judging the tribes of Israel, of witnessing to the age of the Spirit, and of offering forgiveness to all who had been guilty of the blood of Abel. The universal implications of Jesus' mission were being illustrated within the time and space of a single day in the life of the apostles.

This story not only fulfilled earlier commands and predictions but also articulated new predictions that shaped later narratives. Here the story of the council's efforts to kill the apostles marked the first break in the solid front of opposition. The efforts prompted a warning from one of the members of the council, Gamaliel. This break was followed up in at least two specific texts. Soon the narrator observed that "a great many of the priests became obedient to the faith" (Acts 6:7). More significantly, one of Gamaliel's students, the man Saul, in carrying out orders from the high priest to persecute believers, became obedient to the orders of the Spirit and consequently himself became a victim of persecution (22:3–5). That later reversal in Luke's story was a clear fulfillment of Gamaliel's warning: "Keep away from these men . . . if this plan . . . is of God, you will not be able to overthrow them" (5:38–39). To Luke's readers, Gamaliel's warning gave voice to the futility of resisting the Holy Spirit. Thus wherever in Luke-Acts one comes across the trail of Abel's blood, one also comes across the trail of Cain's forgiveness—a major accent in this narrative theology.

That is clearly the case in the story of the appointment of the seven deacons. The selection of the seven marked the first extension of the mission of the apostles to a circle of prophets who had been filled with the Spirit (6:3, 5). This circle included at least one proselyte, who fulfilled one of the Pentecost prophecies (2:10). Hereafter the roster of prophets included spokespersons from the whole house of Israel: Jews by physical descent from Abraham and Gentiles by conversion and circumcision.

The work of these prophets provoked the same confrontation that Jesus and Peter had aroused. On the one hand were prophets acting as exemplars of the grace, power, wisdom, and spirit of the new age (6:8, 10); on the other were synagogue leaders from the Diaspora, as well as from Jerusalem, presenting to the council charges of "blasphemous words against Moses and God" (6:11). Thus the narrator set the stage for Stephen's long summary of Israel's history, which reached its climax in an inflammatory attack on his accusers: "You stiff-necked people, uncircumcised in heart and ears, you are forever opposing the Holy Spirit, just as your ancestors used to do. Which of the prophets did your ancestors not persecute? They killed those who foretold the coming of the Righteous One, and now you have become his betrayers and murderers" (7:51–52). The accusation led to an explosion of hatred and to Stephen's death by stoning. But the narrator was chiefly concerned with accenting four things: the martyr's vision of Jesus at God's right hand, his prayer to Jesus to receive his spirit, his prayer for the forgiveness of his enemies, and the remark that Saul stood among the assassins (7:54–58).

Those accents justify some specific inferences: (1) Jesus' forgiveness of these assassins, because their violence linked them to the entire succession of God's enemies from the beginning (Luke 11:42–52), must have been more powerful and primal than the entire history of such enmity.

(2) A specific instance of this forgiveness in the narrator's mind was the story of Saul, who had approved the murder of Stephen. Saul had a similar vision of the risen Lord (Acts 9:1–5) that conveyed not only his own forgiveness but a call to become a successor to Stephen. Perhaps this was the narrator's way of describing in narrative form what Paul spoke of as predestination (Gal. 1:13–16).

(3) One may see the story of Stephen, taken as a whole, as another example of the first curse in Genesis 3, the curse of a continuing enmity between the seed of the serpent and the seed of the woman— and God's termination of that curse. Further, one may see Stephen's death as a continuation of that curse on Adam, the return of earth to the earth. But if Stephen's prayer was answered, his death also marked a lifting of that very curse. In Stephen's witness, as in the cross of Jesus, the two ages met.

(4) Luke's report of Philip's work in Samaria suggests that a fourth inference may be drawn from Stephen's death. Stephen's example emboldened Philip, in spite of the obvious dangers, to continue proclaiming the crucified Messiah and casting out evil spirits. Even before Philip received Peter's imprimatur, his message evoked the same signs and the same joy that everywhere marked the advent of the new age (8:7–8). When Peter and John arrived, they recognized these signs by conferring the Holy Spirit on the new believers. This Spirit enabled Peter to read the heart of Simon Magus to detect there "the chains of wickedness" that had induced Simon to offer to buy the charismatic authority of the apostles (8:17–24).

Each extension of the movement reflected the powerful guidance of the Holy Spirit. Peter followed such guidance in his response to the Spirit's selection of Cornelius, the Gentile centurion (10:34–48). So, too, when Paul came under attack from Jewish Christians for his Gentile campaigns, Peter was the first to speak in his defense. In saving Gentiles God had erased all distinctions between "them and us." By the grace released through Jesus, God had restored the human situation to what it had been before any division between Jews and Gentiles.

Luke's outlook also permeates the three accounts of Paul's transformation from Christ's enemy to his slave. In the first account the risen Lord told Ananias of his purpose in selecting Paul and declared how he would himself show Paul how much "he must suffer for the sake of my name" (9:16). The Lord thus assigned to Paul the same necessity that Jesus had himself accepted. In the second account Ananias made clear to Paul that it was the God of Abraham, Isaac, and Jacob who had chosen him "to know his will, to see the Righteous One and to hear his own voice," so that Paul could become his witness to the whole world (22:14–15). There could have been no higher authority and no more inclusive mandate.

Luke was even more explicit in his third account of Paul's vision, audition, and commission. What God had done had been in full accord with what the prophets and Moses had said would take place, including three specific points: first, the necessity of the Messiah's suffering (thus linking Paul's suffering to Christ's and fulfilling Jesus' earlier announcement to his disciples); second, the distinctive role of the Messiah in being the *first* to rise from the dead (implying the link between his resurrection and theirs); third, the Messiah's gift of *light* both to Jews and to Gentiles (implying the link of this suffering and vindication with the primal summoning of light out of darkness). Although these were Paul's own words to Agrippa, they were based on words addressed to Paul by the risen Lord himself: "I am sending you to open their eyes so that they may turn from darkness to light, to turn from the authority of Satan to God, to receive forgiveness of their sins, and to receive an inheritance among those who have been made holy by their faith in me" (26:17–18, my trans.). One should not ignore the resonance here of the Genesis traditions. "From darkness to light" reminded readers of God's primal word. "From the authority of Satan" signaled the release from primal captivity. "Forgiveness of sins" pointed to the lifting of the primal curse. "To receive an inheritance" assured the penitent of a final homecoming. Such was the gift and such the commission from the one whose birth had been announced to the shepherds.

Basic Responses

Perceptive readers will, I trust, have sensed my determination to give an accurate exposition of the theological implications in Luke's narratives. In the course of this exposition I have unearthed more evidence than I expected to find to support the conclusion that Luke's thought was impregnated with a profound awareness of the miraculous actualities of the new age wherever he detected the powerful interventions of God's Word and Spirit, and that his narratives of these interventions were subtly shaped by the Genesis traditions of Creation and Fall.

I want now to indicate why I think these considerations might be important to readers and interpreters of the scriptures. I suggest five major areas that may change a reader's response to these two volumes.

First, as in reading any other great literature, one needs to become acutely aware of the author's distinctive vocabulary, that basic repertoire of images and symbols with their original rhythms and resonances. It is obvious that Luke relied on simple, ordinary words familiar to everyone; but it is also clear that he used those words to convey thinking that was indigenous to residents of the new creation. To those recipients of grace, the events centering in the story of Jesus had endowed the simple words with vastly new meanings, meanings appropriate to the world of angels and prophets, of prayers and doxologies. In that world each ordinary word received a new stamp. It was born again as a medium for messages back and forth from human hearts to the imagined world of curses and blessings, humiliations and exaltations.

Consider one example, the use of the word "virgin" in the story of Mary. To residents of the old age, that use of the word seemed incredible and even scandalous, but to residents of the new age it became a natural way, though no less miraculous, to speak of God's intervention in the universal human story through his powerful Word and Spirit. When modern readers grasp the original overtones of the word "virgin" within the context of Gabriel's address to Mary, they are freed from many of the historical and dogmatic hassles that have bedeviled later interpretations. By the same token, Luke is also freed from responsibility for later misinterpretations; he can speak again to his readers in a conversation closer to the original one. What is true of "virgin" is true of other words in Luke's vocabulary.

Second, Luke was primarily a teller of stories; his theology was a narrative theology. Accordingly, in these two volumes, readers should find encouragement to become in their own way tellers of stories and narrative theologians. One looks in vain in Luke-Acts for explicit doctrinal formulations of essential Christian beliefs, but everywhere one detects the activity of God, along with the activity of God's invisible adversary. Damnation and salvation are clearly portrayed as the outcome of those contests for dominance over human hearts. When readers find those contests depicted in the interlocking stories in the Gospel, they are encouraged to discern similar contests proceeding on Main Street and in First Church. When they reflect on the origin of these continuing battles, they may be more likely to find in them an echo of God's curses on Eve and on Cain, as well as an opportunity for the blood of Christ to speak a better word than the blood of Abel. Should they hear this echo, the stories of the last evening Jesus spent with his disciples would recover some of their primal meanings, such as God's removal of the curse through the covenant in the Messiah's blood. Then, the final petition in the Lord's Prayer might again be heard as a cry of desperation: "Do not bring us to the time of trial, but rescue us from the evil one." A cry like that turns all theology into narrative theology and turns every theologian into a storyteller.

Third, the study should make one more adept in understanding and interpreting biblical protology. In scripture, the character of both ages, old and new, was bound up in the origins of both. Disciplined imagination attributed to God's forethought and design not only the depth of alienation in the old but also the promise of liberation into the new. As in 2 Esdras, narrative theology found a decisive and a universal significance in the many *beforenesses* of God's activity. Affirmations of these priorities were neither naive archaeological efforts to recover a primeval past nor astronomical efforts to penetrate to a realm beyond the planets. Rather, they were disciplined and sophisticated ways of visualizing the elemental and universal components in each conflict situation that God's people confronted. These affirmations traced to their ultimate hidden origins the priorities involved in current dilemmas and choices, whether the reference in a specific case was to God's action *before* Moses or Abraham or Babel or Adam. Prophets discerned clues to the end by revelation of the beginning, and the vision of both illuminated the decisions of the moment. Or, rather, prophets brought messages from a "lord" who as "the living one" was himself primal creator and final judge.

Each message, so delivered, was designed as vocational guidance. Thus the vocation of the shepherd-elder in the Ephesian church was linked to the story of Abel, the shepherd, through the story of Jesus, the shepherd. The announcement of the angel to the Bethlehem shepherds provided a visionary *beforeness* to all the later stories Luke told. To Luke, of course, this vision of a prior heavenly design was more than an intriguing literary device; he discerned in what had happened in his own days a consummation of the angel's promise of peace to those whom God favors. Modern sophistication allows to his modern readers little room for such protological fancies. Actually, however, anyone who tries to explain particular *afters* becomes aware of particular *befores*. Before gratitude, the gift; before hope, the promise. The more substantial the *after*, the more definitive its *before*. Obedience recognizes a prior command, as the sense of guilt testifies to the reality of a command rejected. Conscious choices are responses to hidden impulses, whether good or evil; they illustrate continuing cycles, whether vicious or gracious. Birth implies conception, as the existence of a community implies a covenant. So it is that all action points to protological origins, as elemental and essential as the roots of a tree. Luke's stories help readers recover their roots as Christians.

More specifically, Luke may help ministers recover a valid way of thinking about the origins of their own calling as shepherds. Shepherding requires announcing the good news in a world where, as the Genesis story made clear, one cannot separate sin and mortality— or forgiveness and immortality. Where God's blessing displaced his curse, there, too, he shared his life fully with the descendants of Adam. Shepherds stand at this mysterious junction between curse and blessing, judgment and grace, death and life. It is their task to repeat Jesus' warning and promise, fully conscious of its awesome dimensions: "Those who want [like Adam] to save their life will lose it. Those who lose their life for my sake will save it" (Luke 9:24).

Fourth, interpreters of Luke-Acts can all learn from the clear and consistent focus of the narrator's concern. In the Gospel, all stories point ahead to the passion story: "The Son of Man must suffer"; in the

Acts, all stories point back to that suffering as releasing God's creative and redemptive power. It was in that climactic story that Jesus' intercession for his disciples in the upper room exerted the power to bring them after his death to repentance and to include them in his gift of the Spirit. It was from the cross that Jesus' prayer for his adversaries produced a powerful answer in the conversion of priests and the radical transformation of Saul the Pharisee into Paul the slave of Christ. On the cross Jesus' reply to his fellow convict assured him of immediate access to paradise. Thus the suffering of the Son of Man offered example after example of repentance and forgiveness, beginning from Jerusalem and reaching out beyond the pages of scripture. Paul had written of "the law of the Spirit of life in Christ Jesus"; Luke told stories of how that Spirit created a community in which an Ethiopian and a centurion could find immediate welcome, but from which Ananias and his wife found immediate exclusion. Luke gave to the risen Messiah awesome authority over salvation and damnation; interpreters should not diminish such authority.

Fifth, I want to mention a dilemma that interpreters of Luke face. They have mastered the intertextual richness of this author's vocabulary, with its vast penumbra of overtones from all segments of scripture, the overtones of such words as virgin, shepherds, curses, blessings, angels, blood. They have become thoroughly conversant with the perspectives of a narrative theology that embodies the truth in stories, especially the story of Jesus' death and vindication. The more fully they qualify as interpreters, however, the more fully they place themselves under the scrutiny of the original narrator. Luke conducts his own quiet interrogation of all would-be interpreters. When he tells the story of the angels' message to the shepherds, he asks the interpreters whether they are fully aware of the newness and the goodness of that message. Have they done full justice to the shift in the balance of power between the serpent and Christ, Satan and God? Have they recognized the multiple ways in which the message of the angels represents a radically new beginning and a radically new end? Has the message bound them into solidarity with "all the people" in such a way as to reflect the inclusivenes of God's grace? Apart from positive answers to such questions, Luke would have every right to deny interpreters any license to introduce others into his world.

For those who fail this test, Luke made a place within the plot. Their continued residence in the old age was voiced by the Emmaus-bound disciples: "We had hoped . . ." (Luke 2:38; 24:11). Yet it was those same unbelievers who announced a few days later to those who had killed "the Author of life": "There is salvation in no one else" (Acts 4:12). That remains their declaration, a declaration that Luke endorsed for his readers: salvation through one who as son of Adam accepted the archetypal curses and one who as Son of God mediated the blessings of the Almighty.

Notes

1. Søren Kierkegaard, *The Present Age,* trans. Walter Lowrie (New York: Oxford University Press, 1940), 97.

2. Susan R. Garrett, *Demise of the Devil* (Minneapolis: Fortress, 1989), 37.

3. John Milton, *Paradise Lost* (New York: New American Library, 1961), 12.427–34.

3
Adam and Christ

Death and Life in
1 Corinthians 15

What happened in the beginning of days constantly repeats itself in every generation and in the individual.[1]

In reading any ancient document, the laws of intellectual inertia dictate that our first impulse is to insert the new material into our previous thought world, making only minor adjustments to accommodate the new data. Our conceptual world is constructed around an infrastructure of basic perceptions, the latitude and longitude of our mental maps, and these perceptions resist change. Thus on reading an ancient author we do not distort the integrity of that author's thought so long as the author's infrastructure is compatible with ours. But when the infrastructures differ, it is almost inevitable that we do violence, usually unwittingly, to the basic thought patterns of the ancient author. Such violence almost always occurs when those patterns are radically different, when, for example, they assign radically different meanings to the terms "death" and "life."

Such violence in the act of reading we can observe within our own minds when we read 1 Corinthians 15. It is not due simply to the fact that Paul had different ideas from ours about the probability of life after death. Rather it is the fact that such differences reflect different worlds of experience, thought, and language. In reading this chapter, therefore, our first inclination is to retain our previous horizons, making only minuscule adjustments in absorbing the thrust of Paul's logic. But to the extent that we adopt the infrastructure of Paul's thinking about death and resurrection, we alienate ourselves from our previous thought world. When we find the cost of migration too high, our views of life and death usually become a confused palimpsest of two discordant maps.

Such confusion is not limited to modern readers of ancient authors. It was equally present when this letter from the apostle was first opened at a meeting of the congregation in Corinth. Every chapter in that letter provides evidence that their understandings of the gospel varied so widely from his that he was forced to challenge their knowledge of God. Indeed, chapter 15 makes clear that author and readers had drawn contradictory inferences from his earlier announcements of the death and resurrection of their common Lord. Their different perspectives had given very different weights to such mapmaking terms as "earth," "heaven," "body," "spirit," "the first," "the last." In many ways Corinthian perception of those terms coincided more closely with prevalent modern perceptions than with Paul's. Thus on many of the points under discussion in the chapter, modern readers instinctively side with Paul's opponents—and make similar mistakes.

The recognition of substantial divergences between the author and his first readers should not be pressed too far. He was after all the apostle whose message had converted most of them. He had planted the seed, and their existence as a Christian community had been God's harvest of the crop (3:5–9). He gave thanks to God for the many gifts of grace they had received (1:2–9). He assumed that they held firmly to the faith that God had raised Jesus from the dead, for they had been "buried with him by baptism into death" (Rom. 6:3–11). He addressed them as people "sanctified in Christ Jesus." When he dictated 1 Corinthians 15, he was a father addressing his family, not a philosopher addressing a general audience concerning the possibility of postmortem existence. He was seeking to answer serious questions that had been raised in all sincerity within that family. Father and family were bound together by the faith, hope, and love that he had described so profoundly in chapter 13, though not all of them grasped the full implications of those bonds. In short, they had a basis for mental rapport that is often lacking in his modern readership. One objective in studying the chapter, then, is to recapture the strength of those bonds.

I begin this study with the opening verses.

> Now I would remind you, brothers and sisters, of the good news that I proclaimed to you, which you in turn received, in which also you stand, through which also you are being saved, if you hold firmly to the message that I have proclaimed to you—unless you have come to believe in vain. (vv. 1–2)

These verses indicate a major reason why Paul wrote the letter. He was afraid that some readers might have come "to believe in vain." Again at the end of the chapter, Paul expressed his hope that "in the Lord your labor is not in vain" (v. 58). In his discussion, the danger of futility in faith recurs frequently (vv. 10, 14, 17, 32). Indeed, one can view the chapter as a song with this warning as a refrain. Paul's message was at stake. Their faith was at stake. At stake also was their forgiveness through the grace of God. "To believe in vain" meant living in a creation still cursed by God. No wonder that Paul reacted so sharply to their skepticism about the resurrection. To him the implication was clear. If their skepticism was justified, "we are of all people most to be pitied" (v. 19). Faith in Christ's victory over sin and death would have been sheer fantasy (v. 32). With so much at stake, it was natural for Paul to begin his argument by trying to establish agreement on matters "of first importance."

> For I handed on to you as of first importance what I in turn had received: that Christ died for our sins in accordance with the scriptures, and that he was buried, and that he was raised on the third day in accordance with the scriptures, and that he appeared to Cephas, then to the twelve. Then he appeared to more than five hundred brothers and sisters at one time, most of whom are still alive, though some have died. Then he appeared to James, then to all the apostles. Last of all, as to one untimely born, he appeared also to me. For I am the least of the apostles, unfit to be called an apostle, because I persecuted the church of God. But by the grace of God I am what I am, and his grace toward me has not been in vain. On the contrary, I worked harder than any of them—though it was not I, but the grace of God that is with me. Whether then it was I or they, so we proclaim and so you have come to believe.
>
> (vv. 3–11)

In this terse and compact paragraph Paul brought together three worlds that had originally been quite separate: the gospel he had received, his own firsthand experience of revolution, and the Corinthians' experiences in responding to his proclamation. The first of those worlds had originally been independent of both Paul and the Corinthians: the death of Jesus, his resurrection and, his commissioning of Cephas and the other apostles.

That world and Paul's world had converged when "last of all . . . he appeared also to me." That meeting had marked a collision of mammoth proportions. In two laconic verses he summed up a large segment of his own story, his persecution of "the church of God" and his work as an apostle, mediating the grace of God. He tells elsewhere that this persecution had been motivated by love for the scriptures: "as to the law a Pharisee, as to zeal a persecutor" (Phil. 3:6). With the high priest, he had been confident that this messianic claimant had died not for the sins of others but for his own sin, so that apostolic claims that God had glorified Jesus were nothing short of a blasphemy that must be punished by death as ordered by the same scriptures. Such zeal had been sin, however, a sin that God had forgiven when the glorified Messiah had appeared to Paul with an assurance of grace and a new vocation to mediate that grace to others. That revolution had conveyed a radically new understanding of the scriptures and a totally different way of thinking about life and death.

It was into this new world of the gospel that Paul had inducted his Corinthian converts: "so we proclaim, and so you have come to believe" (1 Cor. 15:11). They had experienced a similar kind of inner revolution, elicited by the same grace of God. Their world now overlapped the other two worlds, as signified by the dramatic personal pronoun "our": "Christ died for *our* sins in accordance with the scriptures." The event of Christ's death had established the convergence of three worlds: that of Christ, of Paul, of the Corinthians.

That word "scriptures" marked the presence of a fourth world. The scriptures that once had demanded that Paul persecute followers of the Messiah, by demanding Jesus' own vicarious death, had now opened the way for the resurrection and the declaration of God's grace. Did Paul have in mind some specific text from the Law and the Prophets? Here scholars speak with considerable diffidence. Paul may have had many passages in mind, texts from Deuteronomy, the Psalms, Isaiah, or Ezekiel. But he definitely had *one* text in mind, because he mentioned it as a pivotal point in his argument—the story in Genesis 3, the first book of Moses (1 Cor. 15:21–22).

To recapture Paul's thought, then, one must try to comprehend the convergence and divergence of these four worlds. Thus our next step is to examine the chapter, looking for clues to the position taken by these Corinthian readers.

> Now if Christ is proclaimed as raised from the dead, how can some of you say there is no resurrection of the dead? If there is no resurrection of the dead, then Christ has not been raised; and if Christ has not been raised, then our proclamation has been in vain and your faith has been in vain. We are even found to be misrepresenting God, because we testified of God that he raised Christ—whom he did not raise if it is true that the dead are not raised. For if the dead are not raised, then Christ has not been raised. If Christ has not been raised, your faith is futile and you are still in your sins. Then those also who have died in Christ have perished. If for this life only we have hoped in Christ, we are of all people most to be pitied. (vv. 12–19)

This text offers the earliest direct indication of the position of Paul's adversaries within the Corinthian church, so one must scrutinize it carefully, to note the points of agreement and of disagreement. He may have misread their position (probably conveyed to him by a traveler or a letter), but since the objective here is to grasp Paul's line of reasoning, in this essay I accept his reading of their minds.

There can be no doubt that Paul was addressing Christians, for he speaks of "some of you" (v. 12) and "your faith" (v. 17). Their immediate problem was not the demise of people in general but the death of fellow believers: "those who have died *in Christ*" (v. 18). He does not tell the circumstances of these deaths, but all churches at the time faced unusual rigors of economic discrimination, social ostracism, and even violent pogroms. Thus the fact of being "in Christ" may well have been one of the causes of death. But whatever such causes, these survivors believed that there was no resurrection for their friends who had "fallen asleep." (The situation recalls 1 Thessalonians 4.)

As Paul sets forth the situation, it becomes clear that, although he disagreed with his readers on this point, they agreed on two basic beliefs. In accepting Paul's gospel (1 Cor. 15:11), they had accepted the actuality of the resurrection of Christ from the dead, and they believed, as a corollary, that God had forgiven their sins. Paul had adroitly composed the preceding paragraph to clarify this common ground. He had also anticipated what was at stake by mentioning Christ's burial and the death of some of the first witnesses to Christ's resurrection who had also "fallen asleep" (v. 6).

These two agreements on Christ's resurrection and on the forgiveness of sins provided the basis for Paul to emphasize two contradictions in their position. First, as Paul saw the matter, although they believed in the resurrection of Christ *from* the dead, they disbelieved in the resurrection *of* the dead, that is, of those who had died "in Christ." Paul insisted, on the contrary, that those two resurrections were interdependent. If there were no resurrection *of* the dead there could be no resurrection of Christ *from* the dead (and vice versa). Although the reason why the Corinthian readers distinguished these two resurrections is not known, they may have been following an early tradition that believed that when God raised Jesus from the dead, he did not allow "his Holy One to experience corruption" (Acts 13:33–37), an immunity not granted to all of the faithful.

Second, although they believed in the forgiveness of their sins through Christ's vicarious sacrifice, they did not believe that this forgiveness assured a victory over death by those forgiven. Here, too, Paul detected an intolerable contradiction. If those who die in Christ are not raised (with its corollary that Christ has not been raised), then "you are still in your sins" (1 Cor. 15:16–17). To Paul, Adam's fall had resulted in such a bonding between sin and death that only a cancellation of the curse of death could yield genuine forgiveness of sins. The restriction of forgiveness "to this life only" (v. 19) constituted a total misunderstanding of sins, of forgiveness, of the death of Christ, and of a shared victory over death through the grace of God. For the apostle, these contradictions threatened much more than the Corinthians assumed.

How did the apostle deal with those two contradictions? It was not sufficient simply to assert them. To convince his readers of the untenability of their position, he would have to show how Christ's death and victory over death were related to a victory over death for his followers, and how the forgiveness of their sins depended on their own victory over death. And that is what he proceeded to do, by a new declaration of the good news and by linking that declaration to the scriptures.

> But in fact Christ has been raised from the dead, the first fruits of those who have died. For since death came through a human being, the resurrection of the dead has also come through a human being; for as all die in Adam, so all will be made alive in Christ.
>
> (1 Cor. 15:20–22)

In these verses the apostle emphasized three points. First, he repeated the basic declaration of the gospel that the Corinthians had accepted—that God had raised Jesus from the dead. Second, he asserted that the risen Christ was the *first fruits,* that is, the first gathering *of* the dead. His resurrection guaranteed the full harvest "of those who have died" (v. 20). The first picking and the full harvest were inseparable. Third, he turned immediately to the scriptures in accordance with which Christ had both died and been raised. This text told the story of Adam's sin and death in Genesis 3.

"Death came through a human being"—not through just anyone, of course, but through Adam. This reference called into the reader's field of vision the entire story of Adam. That account made central the link between death and sin. The Creator had forbidden the first human creatures to eat fruit from the tree of knowledge, warning them that they would die on the day they ate it (Gen. 2:17). Adam and Eve had preferred to accept the assurance of the serpent that they would not die. So they defied God's ban. Paul treated this defiance as primal, archetypal, universal. "Sin came into the world through one man and death came through sin, and so death spread to all because all have sinned"

(Rom. 5:12). Sin was prior to death and the cause of it. It was that steel chain that had made necessary Christ's death for everyone's sins, enabling him in the resurrection to become the first fruits of those who have died with and in him. In him, then, "all will be made alive," including the skeptical Christians in Corinth. Such was Paul's first answer to the question they had raised.

This appeal to the analogy of Adam was much more than a rhetorical ploy to win points in a sparring match, and it was more than a simple comparison of two human beings. There was a cause-effect bond: *"since* death came through a human being, the resurrection of the dead has also come through a human being" (1 Cor. 15:21). Scripture had set a requirement that the gospel had met, if life were to be as universal as death. In one human being, *all;* in another human being, *all.* Paul had come to recognize that the revelation of God through Genesis was more authoritative and relevant than those laws that had induced Paul as a Pharisee to persecute the followers of a Messiah who had been crucified as a sinner.

Here one should notice an apparent conflict within scripture and, indeed, within Genesis itself. According to Genesis 3 the penalty for the sin of Adam had taken the form of a series of curses: on the lying serpent, on Eve, on Adam, on their descendants, and on the earth itself, the earth that in Genesis 1 had been judged to be very good. The curses had reached their climax in the announcement of the return of the dust to the dust, separation from the tree of life, and expulsion from the garden. It was this account in Genesis 3 that spelled out in detail the character of the sin and the dimensions of its punishment and thus provided the foil for Paul's thought in 1 Corinthians 15.

But Genesis also has a different account of Adam's death. According to chapter 5, Adam and Eve had many children and Adam lived to be 930 years old! The serpent would seem to have been right after all in assuring Eve that she would not die as punishment for her disobedience. Thus the same book discloses two radically different definitions of death—one was the multiple signs of a curse on Adam and his descendants in chapter 3, the other was his final demise at age 930. The death announced in chapter 5 had no sting; not so the mortality described so colorfully in chapter 3. Its sting was a sin that produced alienation from God and exile from the garden. It introduced an existence on the earth subject to perennial hunger and unending struggle with thorns and thistles. One of its costs was the first murder of brother by brother. It was this composite of penalties that Paul had in mind when he wrote of sin and of the death that was its penalty. When his adversaries said "death" they probably had in mind what happened at the end of Adam's old age (though the narrator of that event gave no theological weight to that event). Not so, Paul. Such at least is the inference that one may now safely draw from the two questions that the Corinthians had raised:

> How are the dead raised?
> With what kind of body do they come?   (v. 35)

After the human dust has returned to the dust, *how* can it be resuscitated? Bodies that are laid in the tomb are subject to rapid decomposition; with what kind of body, then, do they come from the tomb? The questions make no distinction whatever between the fate of believers and that of nonbelievers, between the righteous and the sinners; all bodies are subject to the same laws. Whenever the phrase "the resurrection of the body" is used, such questions spring to life almost inevitably.

So legitimate do such questions seem that many readers, both ancient and modern, have been repelled by the rudeness of Paul's rejoinder: "You fools!" (v. 36).

What can explain Paul's use of this brutal "fools"? It seems especially shocking when one considers that he had begun the letter by thanking God for the grace shown to these very fools. Was Paul acting here as a role model of the love that is not "irritable or resentful" (13:5)? He had been praising these individuals as his children in the gospel; how then can his use of this expletive be justified? Did it express impatience, malice, or a surgeon's therapeutic scalpel? One who fails to grasp the full force of this ejaculation will not comprehend the following argument.

> What you sow does not come to life unless it dies. And as for what you sow, you do not sow the body that is to be, but a bare seed, perhaps of wheat or of some other grain. But God gives it a body as he has chosen, and to each kind of seed its own body. Not all flesh is alike, but there is one flesh for human beings, another for animals, another for birds, and another for fish. There are both heavenly bodies and earthly bodies, but the glory of the heavenly is one thing, and that of the earthly is another. There is one glory of the sun, and another glory of the moon, and another glory of the stars; indeed, star differs from star in glory. So it is with the resurrection of the dead.   (vv. 36–42)

In following Paul's argument, modern readers often raise three questions and give answers to them that Paul would never have given. These three questions are interdependent, but for the sake of clarity one may examine them separately. What does Paul mean by the act of sowing? How does this sowing give life through dying? How does Paul think of the body that God "chooses" to give?

First, what kind of activity is spoken of as sowing? Because of the two questions asked by the Corinthian "fools," readers often assume that by "sowing" Paul here referred to the act of burying a human corpse. This assumption, however, contradicts all other Pauline uses of this metaphor. Paul's use is entirely clear in the two letters to Corinth. Paul had already used the analogy in describing his first contact with these very readers: "I planted, Apollos watered, but God gave the growth. So neither the one who plants nor the one who waters is anything, but only God who gives the growth" (3:6–7). Here human action in obedience to Christ had been succeeded by divine gift. The sowing had been *Paul's work* in proclaiming the good news; the harvest had been God's choice of a body. In this case that "body" had been the *life granted to the Corinthians* as recipients of God's grace. In his later work also Paul had sown "spiritual good" among them (9:11); that sowing had also yielded life among them.

The same image receives more extensive use in 2 Corinthians 9. Significantly in this second letter, Paul dealt with the same opportunity for sowing that he mentioned as a conclusion to his appeal in 1 Corinthians 15. Basic to both letters is the idea of philanthropy as an act of sowing: to sow bountifully is to reap bountifully (2 Cor. 9:6). The seed that is sown is supplied by a God who scatters seed and who increases the seed for those who sow bountifully; by this means God increases "the harvest of your righteousness" (vv. 9–10). Some aspects of that harvest are specified: meeting the needs of the saints, adding to the glory of God, sharing in the common life, being enriched "in every way" (vv. 11–15). In the idiom of 1 Corinthians 15 it was this kind of sowing that produced such a "body" as God chooses.

Before leaving this use of sowing to symbolize a generous benefaction for the saints in Jerusalem, one should recall two issues about that collection—problems involved in its collection and problems involved in its delivery. Some Gentile Christians were slow to contribute because the recipients would be Jewish Christians, many of whom had bitterly opposed Paul's mission among the Gentiles. In view of this enmity, it is not surprising that Paul encountered some tight fists in Corinth. Moreover, Paul recognized that, in delivering this "peace offering" to the church in Jerusalem, the messengers would encounter great hostility and even physical danger. Indeed, on his next trip to Jerusalem to deliver the collection Paul narrowly avoided a lynching. The act of sowing, then, was not risk free! Such risks were intrinsic to doing "the work of the Lord," which in 1 Corinthians 15:58 was another definition of sowing. Sowing referred to the entire work of grace that began with God's forgiveness, that motivated Paul's mission, that activated the Corinthian generosity, and that produced a diversified but abundant harvest.

One cause for Paul's shocking accusation of folly (1 Cor. 15:36) may lie in the sharp contrast between Corinthian concern with what happened to the bodies of individuals after death and Paul's own conception of sowing. Immediately before making this accusation, Paul had pictured the apostles putting themselves in danger every hour. Paul himself died day after day! He had been engaged, in fact, with fighting wild beasts in Ephesus (a possible echo of the struggle promised in Gen. 3:15 between the descendants of the serpent, the craftiest of the *wild beasts* [3:1], and the descendants of Eve). One can gauge the distance between his conception of death and theirs by this other text from 2 Corinthians: "We are . . . persecuted, but not forsaken; struck down, but not destroyed; always carrying in the body the death of Jesus, so that the life of Jesus may also be made visible in our bodies. For while we live, we are always being given up to death for Jesus' sake, so that the life of Jesus may be made visible in our mortal flesh. So death is at work in us, but life in you" (2 Cor. 4:7-12). To Paul the dying that counted most was "the death of Jesus," a vicarious sacrifice through which "the life of Jesus" became visible in mortal bodies. Where is such death located? *"In us."* Where is such life? *"In you."*

That text provided an answer to the second question: How does this act of sowing produce life through dying? The principle is clear: "What you sow does not come to life unless it dies" (1 Cor. 15:36). But the relationship among the seed, the dying, and the coming to life is not clear. The key in this verse is the verb "come to life." Here it is helpful to study the other uses of this verb *zōopoiein,* which has the basic meaning of "creating life" or of "giving life to." Such is the force of the other uses of the verb in this chapter: "all will *be made alive* in Christ" (v. 22); "the last Adam became a *life-giving* spirit" (v. 45). In early Christian uses, the source of this new creation—following death—is traced to God, to the risen Lord, or to the Holy Spirit (Rom. 4:17, 2 Cor. 3:2-6; John 5:21-24; 1 Peter 3:18; *Epistle of Barnabas* 7.2; *Diognetus* 5.11-17; Hermas, *Similitudes* 9.16.1-7). Typical of many texts is Romans 8:10-11. "But if Christ is in you, though the body is dead because of sin, the Spirit is life because of righteousness. If the Spirit of him who raised Jesus from the dead dwells in you, he who raised Christ from the dead will give life to your mortal bodies also through his Spirit that dwells in you." Paul traced the creation of new life in mortal bodies to the joint action of God, the Spirit, and the risen Christ. Consequently, the verb "to create" or "to give life to" is more of a story than an isolated word; it is a story in which many persons were perceived to share in a complex transformation of death into life.

Now returning to the initial text one may locate the source of much misunderstanding. "What you sow does not come to life." One makes a serious mistake to take too seriously the botanical analogy and suppose that in this case the *life* was native to the seed. When a seed is planted in the soil it sprouts on its own and comes to life in a new form—a grain of wheat producing nothing but wheat. All that is far from the thrust of Paul's concern. The *life* that he was concerned with was the gift of God through Christ. Just as the act of sowing (and dying) involved many participants (God, Christ, the Spirit, the apostles, the believers), so, too, the "coming to life" was far different from the natural germination of a grain of wheat (cf. John 4:37; 12:24–25). Even farther from Paul's mind was any correlation between sowing and the act of burying a friend's corpse. Because the choice of a body belongs to God, the "transubstantiation" of mortal sowing into celestial glory is a mystery that mortals cannot penetrate, and the effort to do so is presumptuous as well as futile.

In his other letter to Corinth Paul writes that this transformation of the seed that is sown is not limited to some moment in the future, following a believer's demise: "And all of us, with unveiled faces, seeing the glory of the Lord as though reflected in a mirror, are being transformed into the same image from one degree of glory to another; for this comes from the Lord, the Spirit" (2 Cor. 3:18).

Moreover, one should try to fathom the perspective from which the following hope is expressed:

> We are afflicted in every way, but not crushed; perplexed, but not driven to despair; persecuted, but not forsaken; struck down, but not destroyed; always carrying in the body the death of Jesus, so that the life of Jesus may also be made visible in our bodies. For while we live, we are always being given up to death for Jesus' sake, so that the life of Jesus may be made visible in our mortal flesh. So death is at work in us, but life in you . . . because we know that the one who raised the Lord Jesus will raise us also with Jesus, and will bring us with you into his presence.   (2 Cor. 4:8–14)

This text makes clear that Paul visualized the coming transformation of mortal bodies through the power of God as being a continuation of the present struggles, with their defeats and victories; the future consummation would bring a single, decisive change in one respect: absence would be replaced by presence, separation by reunion with God, with Jesus, with one another.

All these texts visualize a sowing that proceeds throughout the period of mortal life and a harvest of glory that begins with the new life in Christ. Perhaps a text from Philippians provides the closest parallel to the Corinthians' confession: "But our citizenship is in heaven, and it is from there that we are expecting a Savior, the Lord Jesus Christ. He will transform the body of our humiliation that it may be conformed to the body of his glory, by the power that also enables him to make all things subject to himself" (Phil. 3:20–21).

One may safely conclude, then, that for Paul the time of sowing covered the whole existence of the believers, including the time of their "falling asleep"; similarly, the time of resurrection covered the whole work of Christ "in our mortal flesh," beginning with the baptism into his death and including an ultimate transformation. From first to last the confidence was firm: "What is sown is perishable, what is raised is imperishable" (1 Cor. 15:42). In the first of these two clauses Paul showed his basic agreement with the Corinthian skeptics; in the second he sought to correct their skepticism.

The next step, then, is to survey his answer to the third question: How did Paul think about the character of the "body" that God chooses? In his answer, he continued to speak only of Christians (note "we," vv. 49, 57) and of their inclusion within Christ's resurrection.

> It is sown in dishonor, it is raised in glory. It is sown in weakness, it is raised in power. (v. 43)

The decisive verbs are in the passive that biblical grammarians call a "divine passive" which was adopted to avoid too casual a reference to God. It is God who both sows and raises. In this verse careless readers may suppose that the two terms, "dishonor" and "weakness" describe a human corpse as it is being interred. Not so. The adjectives are not medical but ethical and social; here they refer, as in most Pauline contexts, to the shame and weakness of the cross, to the scandalous manner of the apostles' life, or to the social status of converts to Christ. "God chose what is weak in the world to shame the strong" (1 Cor. 1:26–29). Always in the background of thought is the definition of the glory and power that the story of Jesus had provided: "For our sake God made him to be sin who knew no sin, so that in him we might become the righteousness of God" (2 Cor. 5:21). The story of

Jesus changed the human situation as it had existed since Adam. A paraphrase of the verse makes this intertextual link more apparent: "As the firstborn of God, Jesus did not inherit Adam's legacy of sin and death. But he accepted that legacy as a son of Adam so that we might be rescued from that legacy and become righteous before God. All this was done as God's gift to us. This is new creation." The transformation from sin (the first Adam) to righteousness (the second Adam) accompanies the conversion from shame to glory and from weakness to power. Indeed, Paul viewed the moment of a person's conversion as marking the first day of creation, when God commanded light to shine out of darkness (2 Cor. 4:6).

There follows in the text of 1 Corinthians seven other ways of referring to the same transition:

It is sown:	It is raised:
a physical body	a spiritual body
the first Adam	the last Adam
a living being	a life-giving spirit
the first man or humanity	the second man or humanity
the man from earth	the man from heaven
bearing the image of	bearing the image of
the man of dust	the man of heaven
flesh and blood	God's kingdom

In these contrasts Paul focused attention on the two creations, old and new, and on the two "images" that defined the nature of humanity in the two creations. All descriptions of the transformation were based on the Christian gospel (vv. 3–11) but were shaped to illustrate the antitheses to Genesis. All were designed to turn readers' attention away from the questions of the skeptics. In none of the seven does the act of sowing coincide with the moment of death or with the disposition of a corpse; rather it connotes the entire span of earthly life, from birth to death. The recognition of the mortality of the first Adam is free of morbid or psychotic obsession with death; it views the physical body positively, as a form of God's sowing in spite of its perishability.

The composite description of the resurrection also reflects a similar breadth of view. The pivot between the two creations is not restricted to one moment in time or to a single location in space but transcends those dimensions (2 Cor. 5:14–17). The "raising" happened whenever and wherever the new creation was present. From Paul's vantage point when writing, it was already present: "as *is* the man from heaven, so *are* those who are of heaven." But it is also potential: "we *will also bear* the image of the man of heaven" (1 Cor. 15:48–49).

Here I must discuss the possibility that translators should prefer a different text that comes through an ancient manuscript tradition, a tradition usually considered highly reliable. Instead of expressing a future promise, *"we will also bear,"* this tradition extends a strong exhortation: *"Let us bear* the image of the man of heaven" (v. 49). This reading makes the choice of resurrection open to individuals; they can now decide to bear "the image of the man of heaven." Those who die "in Christ" have already obeyed that injunction. Their "body of humiliation" already has a share in "the body of glory" (2 Cor. 3:18). Since that is so, they are fools to ask, "With what kind of body?" The believer's obedience makes it possible for God to transform the body of humiliation into the body of glory. Such a transformation is, in fact, one of the implications of Paul's conviction that those who have died with Christ have already become members of his body (1 Cor. 12:12, 13).

On the basis of these verses one may suggest how Paul might have answered the famous question of Jesus: "Who do you say that I am?" Among his answers would be "the second Adam . . . the last Adam . . . a life-giving spirit . . . the man of heaven."

The apostle has not, however, finished his argument with the Corinthian skeptics, whose confusion still lurks behind the following verses:

> Listen, I will tell you a mystery! We will not all die, but we will all be changed, in a moment, in the twinkling of an eye, at the last trumpet. For the trumpet will sound, and the dead will be raised imperishable, and we will be changed. For this perishable body must put on imperishability, and this mortal body must put on immortality.
> (15:51–53)

Paul distinguished between two groups of Christians who will hear the blast of the last trumpet: some will have died but some will still be alive. He makes the point that members of both groups will be changed. Why did he disclose this mystery? One cogent answer lies in his desire to refute the supposition that for Christians the decisive change takes place postmortem. The questions of verse 35 were mistaken because, if those who were still alive at Christ's coming must also be changed, then it was their mortality and not their death that required "a life-giving spirit." It was the shared "flesh and blood" that could not inherit God's kingdom.

The next few verses provide another answer, one that accepts as valid the scriptural account of the origins of death.

When this perishable body puts on imperishability, and this mortal body puts on immortality, then the saying that is written will be fulfilled:

> "Death has been swallowed up in victory."
> "Where, O death, is your victory?"
> Where, O death, is your sting?"
>
>   (15:54–57)

Paul appealed ostensibly to two prophets, Isaiah (25:7) and Hosea (13:14). Both were concerned with an ultimate victory not by death but over it. Such a victory required knowledge of death's weakness, its sting. Such knowledge had been disclosed in Genesis 3, where vulnerability to death had been located in two other places—sin and law. The command (law) of God issued to Adam had given the serpent an opening for his deception, which had induced Adam and Eve to challenge God's ban, provoking the verdict of death in which all creation had become corrupted. Forgiveness of sin through God's grace had freed creation from the law and had exercised power over death. Dying for sins, Christ had overcome death in sin; he had been raised "a life-giving spirit" (1 Cor. 15:39), giving life to the mortal bodies of all who belonged to him. Ever since, Paul's shout of thanks (v. 57) has been echoed by poets and hymn writers:

> Ye seed of Israel's chosen race,
> Ye ransomed of the fall,
> Hail him who saves you by his grace
> And crown him lord of all.[2]

In short, Genesis 3 had shown that victory over death could be won only by victory over sin. Such a victory had been granted through Jesus Christ—through his death for our sins (1 Cor. 15:3) and his resurrection for our justification (Rom. 4:25). God had thus granted a share in "the image of the man from heaven" (1 Cor. 15:49) to those who share in "the image of the man of dust" (see Gen. 2:7; 3:19). The dimensions of this victory meant that Paul's gratitude covered far more than the earthly fortunes of an individual. To give thanks was to celebrate the restoration of creation to its primal goodness and to replace God's curses by "a shower of blessings." The action of grace was both primal and final; the act of thanksgiving recognized these elemental, structural, and universal dimensions. Accordingly, the recipients of such grace were under obligation to give thanks always and for everything (1 Thess. 5:18). Paul immediately gave a practical way of expressing that gratitude: to share in the image of the man from heaven by engaging vigorously in "the work of the Lord" (1 Cor. 15:58).

This conclusion to the chapter, however, did not by itself answer fully the urgent questions of the Corinthian skeptics. Here one should return to an earlier phase in the discussion:

> For as all die in Adam, so all will be made alive in Christ. But each in his own order: Christ the first fruits, then at his coming those who belong to Christ. (15:22–23)

Through most of the chapter Paul dealt with the problem of how Christians share in Christ's victory over death. In this paragraph he presented his own hope for all humanity. Again he expressed that hope with simultaneous reference to two worlds, that of Genesis and that of the gospel: "all will be made alive in Christ" (v. 22) "so that God may be all in all" (v. 38). These *alls* embraced a final fulfillment for both Creator and creation. Paul discerned three stages in this work of overcoming the death of all in Adam: "each in his own order" (v. 23).

The first order was the resurrection of the Messiah as the *first fruits,* a carefully chosen metaphor. It anticipated the subsequent analogy of sowing and being made alive. In this "first order" God had been the sower through the self-sacrifice by which Jesus had countered Adam's sin of self-seeking. In being raised as the *first fruits* from that sowing, Jesus was not only the first instance of gathering but also a divine guarantee that the entire harvest would follow.

This harvest then represented a second order in the new creation: "at his coming those who belong to Christ" (v. 23). This group would include those Christians in Corinth who had fallen asleep and who had received such a body as God had chosen (vv. 36–41). This order included all who shared in the sowing and the raising of verses 42–50, thus receiving "the image of the man from heaven" (v. 49). They had been freed from the law and from the sting of death through Christ's forgiveness of their sins, joining Paul in his shout of joy (v. 57). They had accepted the ministry of dying every day, choosing to lose their lives rather than to save them. Because their deaths proved that they belonged to Christ, those very deaths constituted one of Christ's gifts to them, along with both the present and the future (3:21–23). Indeed, Paul now viewed their bodies as already members of Christ's body (6:15; 12:13). Their resurrection with Christ would be vindicated at his coming. They are the harvest of which Christ is the first fruits. Such was Paul's answer both to their conclusion (the dead in Christ are not raised: v. 15:15) and to their skeptical questions (with what kind of body). Not only has Christ been raised *from among* the dead; in and through him God has raised up those who have shared in the same sowing and who have received "the spiritual body" of "the last Adam."

Christ was first fruits in an even larger harvest, not only of those who have died *in him* but also of God's entire creation, which had become subject to competing rulers, authorities, and powers. To Paul, these alternate gods had to be destroyed before the human situation following Genesis 3 could be restored to the situation of Genesis 1.

> Then comes the end, when he hands over the kingdom to God the Father, after he has destroyed every ruler and every authority and power. For he must reign until he has put all his enemies under his feet. The last enemy to be destroyed is death. For "God has put all things in subjection under his feet." But when it says, "All things are put in subjection," it is plain that this does not include the one who put all things in subjection under him. When all things are subjected to him, then the Son himself will also be subjected to the one who put all things in subjection under him, so that God may be all in all.   (15:24–28)

Paul recognized, along with his Corinthian readers, that there was a kingdom ruled by Death. As things stood, God was not "all in all." For this kingdom to be "handed over" to God the Father, these alternative authorities must be brought into subjection.

This perspective has become unintelligible to modern readers, for whom ultimate issues are determined more by wars among nations than by struggles among heavenly powers. We visualize the future in terms of fluctuating reports of human gains and losses, so that our emotions oscillate between relative degrees of optimism and pessimism. We do not readily see how daily fears and hopes reflect the hidden authority of many lords and many gods (1 Cor. 8:6). Not conscious of such subservience, we are unaware of how many authorities and powers must be destroyed before one God can become "all in all." To begin to comprehend Paul's thought we must realize that for him the world before and apart from Christ was described by Genesis 3 and that any escape from that world must be by a return to the dominion described by Genesis 1.

In Paul's world, death was visualized not primarily as something that happened to individuals (as to Adam in Genesis 5) but as a universal and ultimate enemy, one of the rulers competing with God for control over creation. It was a lasting proof of Adam's obedience to the serpent rather than to God, an instrument of captivity to God's permanent enemy, an enemy that must be destroyed before God could be "all in all." The word denoting such a foe of creation should be capitalized: Death.

Paul spoke of this ruler as the "last" enemy. That adjective "last" is capable of conveying several meanings. Obviously it meant a *conclusive* battle in a long war. It also meant victory in an *inclusive* warfare, since this Death was the tool of all the authorities and powers resisting God's rule. The term "last" was also used as the opposite of the "first," the primordial battle that God had lost to this same enemy. The last battle was to the last Adam what the first battle was to the first Adam. That first battle had been lost to the serpent in such a way that the curse on the serpent had remained in force: "I will put enmity between you and the woman, and between your offspring and hers" (Gen. 3:15). Death was the first mark of that enmity: "all die in Adam." Victory over that Death was its last mark.

The power of Death to rule over the offspring of Adam and Eve had been exemplified when their first son had murdered his brother. Cain had thus shown his obedience to one of the gods of this world that blinds his worshipers into engaging in acts of violence (2 Cor. 4:4). Before Paul, Jesus had spoken of the complicity of all the murderers of the prophets in shedding the blood of Abel (Matt. 23:35; Luke 11:49–51). To the evangelists all these deaths, including the crucifixion of Jesus, had been the work of serpents (Matt. 23:33), a brood of vipers linked directly to the first enemy. So, too, for Paul, Death was one of "the rulers of this age" who had "crucified the Lord of glory" (1 Cor. 2:7–8). In that act those rulers had demonstrated the "wisdom of this age." But another wisdom had been hidden from those rulers; had they known it they would not have crucified Jesus. This was a wisdom that God had "decreed *before* the ages for our glory" (2:7). By the death of his Son God would win the battle over his last enemy, Death. Just as the power of the serpent had been demonstrated in the long line of murderers, so the power of God had been demonstrated in the long line of martyrs, the wisdom decreed *before the ages* triumphing over the wisdom of the rulers *of* this age. The *last* enemy was responsible for this longest of all warfares.

The first order in winning victory had been Christ's resurrection; the second order had been the resurrection of those who belong to him (including those Corinthians who had died). The third order Paul expressed in words drawn from Psalm 8: "he must reign until he has put all his enemies under his feet" (1 Cor. 15:25; Ps. 8:6). This figure of reducing enemies to a footstool was a way of identifying a military conqueror and is still used in modern warfare. The psalmist was appealing to the account of creation in Genesis 1. There God had given the human creation the glory and honor of having dominion over animals, birds, and fish, so that God could call everything "very good." There, too, God had exerted authority "to silence the enemy and the avenger" (Ps. 8:2). As a result God's name had been exalted throughout the earth (8:1, 8). Such had been the human situation before sin had intervened with its disruption of Adam's dominion over the earth and Adam had been expelled from the garden—that long description of Death as given in Genesis 3. Such would be the human situation again after the last enemy had been subjected to the wisdom and power of the risen Christ and after Christ had turned the rule of the garden over to God. The secret weapon for accomplishing this revolution was the cross that Paul had proclaimed from the beginning (1 Cor. 1:18–25). The humble self-sacrifice of "a life-giving spirit" had overcome the death-dealing enmity of the serpent.

The questions of the Corinthian skeptics thus provoked a far-reaching answer from their "father" in the gospel. They had been able to believe in Christ's resurrection *from* the dead but not in the resurrection *of* the dead. They could not fathom *how* the dead could be raised. Paul's answer relied on an understanding of the wisdom and the power of the cross in terms of an old age defined by Genesis 3 and of a new age defined by Genesis 1. Because of this power, those who belonged to Christ shared in a double victory over death. By the forgiveness of their sins God had freed them from the law and from the sting of death; he had included them in sowing "the man of dust" and in raising "the man of heaven" (1 Cor. 15:56–59). Now Corinthians by their sowing could participate in the continuing warfare between Christ and the rebellious authorities and share in the defeat of the last enemy, Death (15:26). Having shared in the first victory they could, by continuing in "the work of the Lord" (15:58), share in that final victory as well. "As all die in Adam, so all will be made alive in Christ." To Paul, this was the knowledge of God (15:34) that his readers were in danger of surrendering.

The prophet John in Revelation 20 distinguished these two victories in a comparable fashion. The first victory of Christ over "the ancient serpent" coincided with the death of those martyrs who had been beheaded for giving their testimony to Jesus (20:1–4). The final victory was won when "Death and Hades gave up the dead that were in them and were utterly destroyed" (20:13–15). The double victory made possible a "new heaven and a new earth" (21:1), described in the language of Genesis 1. This perspective was not limited to apocalyptic fantasies. The entire New Testament speaks with a single voice. Looking back to one victory of God's grace over death, the authors announced with confidence a final victory over every hostile ruler, authority, and power.

Notes

1. Søren Kierkegaard, *Edifying Discourses,* trans. David F. Swenson and Lillian M. Swenson (Minneapolis: Augsburg, 1944), 2.29.

2. Edward Perronet (1725–1792), *The Pilgrim Hymnal* (Boston: Pilgrim, 1962), 195.

4
Works of God

The Two Families in
John's Gospel

Christ is the truth. . . . Truth consists not in knowing the truth
but in being the truth. . . . Only then do I truly know the truth
when it becomes a life in me.[1]

The Gospel of John opens with a carefully crafted effort to trace two opposing human families to their invisible but real origins. This effort was
grounded in the conviction that knowledge of such origins would clarify their identities and shape their current decisions. The ultimate origin of one family was traced to the Word or Logos of God: "In the
beginning was the Word" (1:1). That declaration brought into conjunction two magnetic fields of reference, each of which was unlimited
in scope and highly complex in implication. One of these fields was the
account of creation recorded in the first book of Moses; the other was
the account of Jesus that followed in the Gospel itself. The literary
structure of the Prologue was shaped to show this fusion; more significantly, however, the thought structure of the Prologue provided essential clues to the infrastructure of the thinking in the rest of the Gospel.
One of those clues was the emphasis on the distinction between the
prevenient, pretemporal *befores* and the postincarnation *afters*. The title
phrase, "in the beginning," was more than a point of departure for the
narrative, as if it were "once upon a time." It remained the intrinsic
source that would enable readers to understand all that would follow.

In this respect John's thinking was similar to that of 2 Esdras. That
author believed firmly in two ages, in a present evil age and a coming
age. With equal firmness he believed that both ages and the transition
between them were determined by God's design. To understand any
event one must know what God had planned before the "portals of
the world were in place" (2 Esd. 6:1). Esdras listed seven such *befores*,
and his list reached a climax in three: "before the present years were
reckoned and before the imaginations of those who now sin were
estranged, and before those who stored up treasures of faith were

82

sealed" (6:5). These three show that Esdras was primarily concerned with understanding "the present years," and that such a concern was dominant because of the current conflict between the faithful and the sinners. The resolution of that conflict depended on God's design even before the conflict had emerged: "Then I planned these things, and they were made through me alone and not through another; just as the end shall come through me alone and not through another" (6:6). This perspective was for Esdras the necessary corollary of faith in one God, and the author of the Fourth Gospel was as much a monotheist as Esdras.

The Johannine Prologue reflects a similar recognition of the necessity for understanding the divine *befores* if one were to understand the human *afters*. This is surely the reason that John asserted the earliest conceivable origin for the Logos. Not only was the Logos with God, it was God. Because of this identity, all things came into being through the Logos. To make this point doubly certain, John repeated it: Not one thing came into being without the Logos. Then John added an even more emphatic declaration of origins: "What has come into being in him was life"; and then, to sharpen the focus, "the life was the light of all people." These *befores* were essential both to John's vocabulary and to his approach to present events: God, the word, all things, life, light, humankind. This poet, in crafting the Prologue, had one eye fixed on the Genesis account of creation, where these *befores* first appear, and the other eye fixed on the stories about Jesus. At least translators are forced, no later than in verse 10, to translate the pronoun *autos* that initially referred to the Logos by the personal "he." This poet had moved by careful steps from the beginning before all things were made to a human being whom he finally named, Jesus Christ, "God the only Son" (1:17–18).

If the first four verses accented the absolute beginnings, the rest of the poem stressed a double focus on relating the *befores* to "the present years" (2 Esd. 6:5). The double role of John the Baptist was the first example of this double focus. Though Jesus came *after* John, John proclaimed that he had been sent from God to testify that Jesus was *before* him as a pretemporal light. John stressed three things about this light: it was true; it was the primordial universal light; it was appearing in the world as a single human being. In this case, "coming into the world" denoted not Jesus' birth by Mary but John's presentation of him to the world (1:15, 27). So insistent was the narrator on this double focus that he repeated five times the verbal paradox of "after-before" ("He who comes after me was before me"—1:15, 27, 30, 36; 3:29). Priority proved higher authority and wider dominion.

The Prologue contained other examples of this double focus, though they are less visible: "the world came into being through him; yet the world did not know him" (1:10). The world came into being through him, and yet by coming into the world, he appeared after the world, and the world's failure to know him was a mark of its guilt. All this was as if to say "Before the world was, I Am" (cf. 17:5). Or, as another example, "he came to what was his own *[ta idia]*, yet his own did not accept him" (1:11, my trans.). The translation "his own" is accurate, even though it leaves some doubt as to who these people were in demographic terms. In any case, the choice of the term presupposed the priority of the Logos: his own had come into being through him. Yet he came to them after their creation and they should have recognized him. Some did, others did not. To those who did, he gave the authority to become the children of God. The pretemporal light made that gift possible. Again the inference is justified: this was as if Jesus said to his own who accepted him, "Before my own were, I Am." Their life as children of God was to be found in the beginning with God.

Some interpreters have concluded that the Johannine term "his own" referred to the house of Israel, bound together by the law as "given through Moses." It is a truism to say that Jesus came to his own after the time of Moses; the Prologue was in effect asserting "Before Moses was, I Am." Such a conclusion, however, is virtually required if one takes seriously the stress on Jesus as "a father's only Son" and on this Son's gift of "grace upon grace." Grace and truth had come through him and not through the law (v. 17); therefore, the fullness of grace had been present in him prior to the law. Moses and the law had come after the events recounted in Genesis 3, whereas grace and truth opened the way to a return to the situation of Genesis 1, before the serpent's lies had induced Eve and Adam to sin, the act that had prompted the curses of God. Because sin had come into the world before the law, there were sins from which Moses could not offer freedom. But before sin had come, all things had come into being through the Logos, who now made available a fullness of grace instead of curse and of the truth instead of the lie. In accepting him, "his own" became children of God, heirs of the life that "in the beginning" was "in him." They were in fact the Logos generation.

Interpreted thus, the Prologue provides clues to the literary structure of the Gospel that followed. Three major divisions in that structure are commonly observed. The first segment, from chapter 2 through chapter 12, is often called the "Book of Signs." One can read this series of signs as a demonstration of the point made in the Prologue that when the Logos came into the world, the world did not know him. Each sign represented the result of the coming of the Logos to the world. John the Baptist had revealed his status as "the Lamb of God that takes away the sin of the world" (surely an echo of Genesis 3). Similarly, even before Nathaniel had come to Jesus, Jesus had seen him "under the fig tree" as "an Israelite in whom is no deceit" (John 1:47–48). In a similar way the first sign took the form of Jesus providing a later wine for a wedding, one better than the earlier, a wine of whose origin the steward of the feast did not know. Neither did Jesus' mother. This "later" sign of an "earlier" glory helps to explain the brusque, if not cruel, reply of Jesus to her obvious comment. He said, "What have you to do with me?" Such brusqueness called attention to her ignorance of the primal glory of which "the good wine" was a manifestation. It was precisely the revelation of this glory that led disciples to believe in him (2:11).

The second segment, often titled "Farewell Discourses," constituted an expansion of a verse in the Prologue, "to all who received him, who believed in his name, he gave power to become children of God" (1:12). On the human calendar, the date was significant—his hour had come "to go to the Father" (13:1). Knowing that the Father had given all things into his hands (an echo of 1:2), knowing that he had come from God (the ultimate *before*) and was going to God (the ultimate *after*), he loved his own who were in the world and he loved them to the end (13:1). Thus John provided a definition of "his own" and of their place of residence. Their status as "his own" had been built into God's original design. Now Jesus could reveal to them the love that enabled him to call them not servants but friends, members of God's family. Accordingly, readers could overhear in Jesus' closing prayer the fulfillment of the declaration that had been made in the Prologue:

> Father, the hour has come; glorify your Son so that the Son may glorify you, since you have given him authority over all people, to give eternal life to all whom you have given him. This is eternal life, that they may know you, the only true God, and Jesus Christ whom you have sent. I glorified you on earth by finishing the work that you gave me to do. So now, Father, glorify me in your own presence with the glory I had in your presence *before the world existed.*
>
> (17:1–5)

The third segment of the Gospel (chap. 18 through chap. 21) describes in some detail the final struggle between the darkness and the light, as announced in the Prologue (1:5). In accomplishing the death of Jesus, the darkness had realized its goal but had unintentionally demonstrated the victory of the primal light. The *after* of Jesus' death disclosed the *before* of life: "in him was life, and the life was the light of all people." Thus readers can see the grand *inclusio:* at the beginning the announcement of light's victory over the darkness, and at the end the return of the Logos to his primal glory (17:5). Just before that final return, however, the glorified Jesus gave to Mary a message for his disciples: "I am ascending to my Father and to your Father" (20:17). The same Father, the same beginning, the same ending. As Jesus had seen God, so they could say "we have seen his glory" (1:14). As Jesus' sonship was embodied in his being sent, so too, their identity as children of the same Father was embodied in being sent by the glorified Son (20:21). Thus each of the promises in the Prologue provided a preview for a later segment of the Gospel; together those three segments illustrated the primal design: God's love for the world before the world existed.

The correlation between the Prologue and the literary structure of later chapters is impressive; even more impressive is the congruence in patterns of thinking, especially thinking about the two families. To one family the coming of the Logos meant wrath and judgment; to the other it meant eternal life in the one who, like the Father, had life "in himself" (5:26). In tracing these patterns the advice of Esdras is again helpful. When he raised the question as to how the beginnings and the ends of the ages might be detected, he received an important guide. It is in the events of the present that prophets should discern the design of the Most High. One may detect primal beginnings in "wonders and mighty works"; one may detect the ends in "penalties" that are signs of judgment and wrath (2 Esd. 9:5–6). When measured thus, of course, those "times" do not coincide with epochs marked off on human calendars. Seeking, then, to understand John's thinking about the two families, I will observe these "mighty works" and "penalties" in the Book of Signs, selecting for special examination several key dialogues.

In John 3 one notices the recurrence of a Prologue motif, the conflict with darkness that was precipitated by the coming of the light into the world (1:5). Symbolically this motif was signaled by Nicodemus's coming to Jesus by night when he recognized from the signs that Jesus had come from God. The advent of the light polarized the community into a sharp division between those who came to the light and those who refused to come because their works were evil. Such polarization was declared to be the judgment of God (3:19); in other words, behind the responses of people to Jesus, John saw the end as well as the beginning of the "times of the Most High."

A second motif that echoed both the Prologue and the Genesis saga was the observation that those who loved and came to the light had been born from above and born of the Spirit. In this case Nicodemus, the Pharisee, served as the devil's advocate with his protest: "How can anyone be born after having grown old?" The query gave the narrator the opportunity to place the accent again on his truth: what comes later both hides and discloses what had been true earlier. Such was the case with the baptism of the Spirit. Linked in the Genesis epic to the wind that swept over the face of the waters, the Spirit gave birth into the eternal life that was given in God's own Logos. Thus both the beginning (as life) and the ending (as wrath) were present whenever later readers pondered the story. All this was summarized in the verse that millions of readers have since memorized as an epitome of the Gospel. In fact, the verse was simply a reshaping of two verses in the Prologue (1:10, 11). A paraphrase may indicate this congruence and reduce the loss of meaning due to familiarity: "This is the way that God showed his love for the world: he sent into the world his beloved Son, the Logos that had been with God from the beginning and through whom the world had been created, so that those who accept him as God's Son might inherit the life that had been in him from the beginning and so that they might be rescued from the wrath with which God has cursed Adam and his heirs" (3:16). To be born of the Spirit is to enter into this family's inheritance of life and to be rescued from the other family's inheritance of wrath.

Again in chapter 5, in another sign that embodied the presence of both the beginning and the end, John described the polarization. This sign took a double form. First, it was the cure of a man who for thirty-eight years had been helplessly ill, but whom Jesus commanded to stand up (the same Greek verb was used again in v. 21 to indicate God's action in raising the dead). Second, because this act took place on the Sabbath, obedience to Jesus' command appeared to entail violation of Moses' prohibition of work on the Sabbath. Both aspects of the sign provoked persecution of Jesus by the Jews, another instance of Jesus' coming to his own and being rejected.

Jesus' explanation also took a double form that was embodied in his enigmatic declaration: "My Father is still working and I also am working" (5:17). First, this word "working" identified the healing as a sign in which the Father and the Son had joined in a single work. The force of this word *(ergon)* derives in part from its use in Genesis to refer to all that God had done in creation (Gen. 2:2). The Father and the Son were cocreators! The force of the declaration also derives from the Johannine Prologue: "the Word [Logos] was God . . . without him not one thing came into being" (1:13). The union of Father and Son in a single work was so clearly a claim to blasphemous equality with God that it instantly aroused the desire to kill Jesus.

Second, an even more blasphemous assertion was concealed in Jesus' reply. This assertion becomes apparent when one notices the accent on the tense of the two verbs—both are in the continuous present. In this common work, the Father and the Son are *still creating*. Readers may infer from the present tense that this work of healing was taking place during the first six days, *before* the creation of the Sabbath. In the terms of 2 Esdras, in this mighty work of the present one could discern the beginning of the "times of the Most High," a return to paradise. This sign expressed the truth of the Prologue: through the Logos all things came into being, that is, before the Sabbath. Thus Jesus' defense had two parts, and both parts angered the defenders of Moses.

The narrator stressed the importance of Jesus' defense by repeating it in the next paragraph: "The Son can *do* nothing on his own, but only what he sees the Father *doing;* for whatever the Father *does,* the Son *does* likewise"(v. 19). It is easy to miss the force of this little word "do" *(poiein)*. It echoes Genesis 1, where it was regularly used to refer to God's creative deeds: "And God *made.*" In response to the adversaries' protest, Jesus did not modify his earlier assertion; though he could *do* nothing on his own, what he had *done* (created) had been the Father's *deed.* Indeed, Jesus maximized the importance of what he had done. It was more than a gift of health; it was an act of giving eternal life: "Just as the Father raises the dead and gives them life, so also the Son gives life to whomever he wishes" (John 5:21). The Son claimed authority to give eternal life. This work marked both the beginning and the ending of the times because it disclosed not only the creation of life, as in the first days, but also the resurrection of the dead, as at the last judgment.

The narrator thus interpreted the controversy that broke out when Jesus ordered the sick man at Beth-zatha to stand up. Against the background of Genesis and John 1, Jesus had seen the creative action of God and had thereby given life "to whomever he wished." The effect was the same as if Jesus had announced to the Jews, "Before the Sabbath was, I Am." It was also as if he had said, "Before Adam sinned and died, I Am." The narrator thus distinguished two families. One was composed of those who, in hearing Jesus' Logos and in believing that God had sent Jesus, received immediately the gift of eternal life, like the man who had been healed. They had already passed from death (the curse on Adam) to life and would no longer come under the curse assigned to Adam's heirs. These persons were distinguished from the dead who, on hearing the voice of God's Son, would be raised, some to life and some to condemnation (5:25–28). One can suppose that those alive who rejected Jesus' Logos would join the latter as members of the second family. Even in that final judgment (an hour that is coming and is already here), the will of the Son as *judge* would be identical with the will of the Father who had sent him (v. 30).

The narrator brought the debate to a temporary close by showing that as a result of Jesus' sign there had been an inescapable conflict between two views of God's creative works, two responses to the Logos, two human perceptions of eternal life and the final judgment. All these were anchored in two contradictory ways of interpreting the scriptures, the testimony of Moses. To the adversaries, the deeds of Jesus defied the law of Moses; in defense Jesus appealed to that very law: "If you believed Moses, you would believe me, for he wrote about me" (v. 46). In effect Jesus thereby said, "Before Moses was, I Am." The narrator made no effort to ignore or to minimize the impasse; he accepted it as part of God's initial design: "he came to his own and his own did not accept him" (1:11, my trans.).

The struggle between Jesus and "his own" became even more acute in chapter 8; therefore that chapter provides a still more sharply etched portrait of the other family. Genesis 1 had reported the first word of God as the command "Let there be light." John also viewed light as the primal reality, but he made light an expression of the creation of life. Life was primary, light secondary: "What has come into being in him was life, and the life was the light of all people. The light shines in the darkness, and the darkness did not overcome it" (1:3–5). The implication is clear that by shining in the darkness the light had provoked resistance, though this resistance had ultimately proved to be futile. In Moses' account of day one, both light and darkness had been present, but there had been no mention of a struggle between them. In John, the mention of the struggle became a preview of the following chapters.

At the outset of this later debate with the Pharisees, Jesus declared openly, "I am the light of the world. Whoever follows me will never walk in darkness but will have the light of life" (8:12). These lines surely allude to the creation of light on the first day of creation, and even more surely to the Prologue's identification of the light with the life *of* and *in* the Logos. Readers would also sense a reference to beginnings in Jesus' reminder about where he had come from, and a reference to endings in his words "where I am going." The ensuing debate involved ultimate issues.

That debate served to disclose clearly the origins of the two families: one was born from below and the other was born from above, one from the world and the other not from the world (v. 23). Inseparable from the origins were distinct destinies (v. 21). Jesus revealed the destiny of his opponents in words that echoed God's words when he addressed Adam in the garden: "You will die in your sin" (v. 21; cf. Gen. 2:17; 3:3). Ironically, this was precisely the charge of those opponents: Jesus would die because of his sin. But the narrator agreed with Jesus that their death in sin was a direct fulfillment of the Genesis curse; in sharpest contrast was the assurance that Jesus' followers would never see death, because they were freed from the execution of that curse (v. 51).

The contrast between the two destinies corresponded to the two paternities. On the one hand, Jesus reiterated the Prologue's manifesto of the unity of the Logos and God; the words and works of the Son were the words and works of his Father (vv. 16–19, 28–29, 38, 47). So complete was this union that on three occasions Jesus used the revelatory divine name, the eternal present "I Am" (vv. 24, 28, 58). His desires and will and works were the same as his Father's.

The paternity of his accusers was asserted with the same certainty: "You are from your father the devil" (v. 44). The devil was identified as "a liar and the father of lies," surely an allusion to the archetypal lie of the serpent in the deception of Eve (Gen. 3:1, 4). The identification as the father of lies meant that Jesus' enemies had become children of the lie as heirs of Eve and Adam (John 8:44). So, too, the allusion to Genesis appeared in the reference to the devil as "a murderer from the beginning." In Genesis the first execution of God's curse on the serpent had been Cain's murder of Abel (Gen. 4:1–6). Jesus was quite explicit in linking their desire to kill him to the desires of their father, this archetypal murderer. Two fathers, two families, two desires, two sins, two deaths, two beginnings, two endings—all these became visible when this light shone in this darkness and this darkness tried to overcome it. All these reflected a triangular field of magnetic resonance: Genesis, the story of Jesus, and the fusion of the two in the Prologue.

I now turn to an analysis of Jesus' actions and words in John 9. With great economy in words John set the stage. "As he walked along, he saw a man blind from birth. His disciples asked him, 'Rabbi, who sinned, this man or his parents, that he was born blind?'" (vv. 1–2). This setting focused attention on three terms: birth, sin, blindness. Each posed a problem of understanding, a problem that recurs throughout the chapter. To understand each of the three terms required understanding the other two. The very act of posing the question carried various implications. When raised by disciples, the question implied faith in the authority of his answer. It implied that this rabbi had access to the truth about birth, about sin, about blindness, a truth that is not fully revealed until the very end of the chapter. It implied both the insufficiency of their own knowledge and the sufficiency of his. It thus fed the expectation that his answer would disclose new meanings in each of the three terms.

Interest was thus focused on him and his answers. John did not focus interest on the blind man, his earlier years, his previous behavior, the character of his parents, or the conditions of his birth. Nor did John concentrate on the actuality of the healing; a challenge to its actuality was quickly dismissed when the parents readily established that he had been born blind. In this episode John shows little interest in the disciples—what led them to pose this question or what was their connection to the other actors. The question focused on the verbal answer of Jesus and on the resulting debates with the Pharisees. It is a strange fact that John did not even mention a request for Jesus to heal the beggar. Jesus did not disappoint his disciples: his words were reported as if they carried authority, as if they represented the design of God that the disciples were bound to accept. He did not evade the question but answered it succinctly and followed it with an alternative that the disciples had not considered: "Neither this man nor his parents sinned; he was born blind so that God's works might be revealed in him" (v. 3). Jesus shifted the discussion to a new direction. He peremptorily rejected both explanations that the disciples had considered and announced a totally different one.

What lay back of this blindness was a design of God, a divine foreknowledge about which John assumed that Jesus could speak with confidence. The priority and power of such a design had been fully stated in the Prologue. The fact of such a design had been attested by John the Baptist. It had been illustrated in Jesus' word of welcome to Nathaniel. It had been strongly argued by Jesus in his debate with Nicodemus. It had been demonstrated in earlier acts of healing. The all-knowing God had a purpose for this very occasion, and Jesus was privy to that purpose (an implicit recognition of the reality of divine election).

In the case of the blind man, this purpose was clearly specified: to disclose God's works. That was no new or strange idea, for the evangelist had referred to those works in virtually every chapter since the debate with Nicodemus. Time after time God's works had been accomplished through the works of Jesus (4:34; 5:17, 36; 6:27–29). A claim to that effect by Jesus had released deadly hostility on the part of adversaries, for whom it was tantamount to claiming a blasphemous equality with God (5:17–18). In his response, Jesus had argued that while his works were the works of his Father, their own works were the works of their father, the devil (8:39–47). The works of God in Jesus simply exposed the works of the devil in them. God's work in the blind man included far more than simply the gift of sight. Because this gift had been designed before his birth, his sight revealed a prior birth as a child of God (1:13). That work was not complete until the blind man had come to faith in Jesus as God's coworker, and until he had accepted the assignment from Jesus expressed in the word "Sent." That work then led to his risky confrontation with Jesus' opponents. Thus Jesus' work as the light of the world brought the beggar out of the world of darkness, the world of sin and death. "God's works" in the vocabulary of John was a code word that identified the invisible actors in the conflict that had been provoked by Jesus' obedience to God's will (5:36–38; 6:28–33). Or as John wrote: "Just as the Father has life in himself, so he has granted the Son also to have life in himself" (5:26).

Thus the sight given to the blind man was correlated to light and hence to life: a correlation that invited readers to recall the Prologue, with its tracing of light to its source: "What has come into being in him was life, and the life was the light of all people" (1:3–4). Thus the sight that was given to the blind man was a work of God that could be traced to this light, and thereby to this life, and thereby to this God. As the author of 2 Esdras had written, one purpose in God's creation of light had been so that his works might be seen (6:39–40); another purpose was this: "all shall see what has been destined" (7:42).

But the phrase "God's works" could also be traced behind the Prologue to the Genesis story of creation with its understanding of the role of God's Word and Spirit as the source of light and life. Summing up the work of God during the first six days are these words: "On the seventh day God finished the *work* that he had done, and he rested on the seventh day from all the *work* that he had done" (Gen. 2:2). Indeed, John probably had the very first day in mind, for later on he used the explicit declaration: "Never since the world began" (John 9:32). He was not alone among early Christian writers in thinking of the works of God as what had been accomplished during the first week (Heb. 1:10; 4:3–4). This conception of the works of God was part of Jesus' defense against the charge of violating the Sabbath both here (9:16) and in the earlier controversy over God's works (5:10–18).

That controversy centered in the claim that Jesus was doing God's works: "We must work the works of him who sent me while it is day; night is coming when no one can work. As long as I am in the world, I am the light of the world" (vv. 4–5). These verses clearly identified the work of Jesus in healing the blind man with God's works; this identification was indicated by Jesus' use of the pronoun "we." In this one work the Father and the Son shared (for a similar use of the first person plural, see 10:30; 14:8–11, 23; 17:11, 21–22). Such an identification prompted Jesus' opponents to reject him, since it claimed an equality with God that was blasphemous. This rejection proved their blindness, their inability to see the light, and their alienation from life (the correlation of blindness/darkness/sin/death was the alternative to sight/light/freedom from sin/life). Thus the blindness expressed their fulfillment of the Prologue: "He was in the world, and the world came into being through him; yet the world did not know him" (1:10). The first words of God had been "Let there be light." Now their blindness was a tragic sign of the presence of that light: "I came into the world for judgment . . . that those who see may become blind" (9:39). The work of God had become not only an act of creation but simultaneously an act of judgment, an act that fulfilled the announcement of the Prologue. Their blindness represented a misunderstanding of that very law of Moses which they were pledged to obey and to teach (9:28).

One may detect another subtle allusion to Genesis: "When he had said this, he spat on the ground and made mud with the saliva and spread the mud on the man's eyes, saying to him, 'Go, wash in the Pool of Siloam' (which means Sent). The man went and washed and came back able to see" (vv. 6–7). John seems to have taken a special interest in this use of mud. There are other stories of healing the blind, but this detail does not appear in any of them. Moreover, John refers to the mud four times, suggesting both special emphasis and the presence of symbolic nuances. Recalling how God and Jesus joined in the work of giving life, one may detect here a reminder of God making Adam out of the dust of the ground (Gen. 2:7; 3:19). Thus Jesus by making mud shares in the work of new creation, for the gift of sight was a form of giving life. (The verb in Genesis is the same verb as John used: "to make," *poiein*.) The command to wash also occurs four times; the act seems to have been necessary for the cure. Here interpreters are fond of discerning an allusion to baptism, with its association of a new birth of water and the Spirit (e.g., John 3:4). John had already linked that Spirit to the wind sweeping over the waters in day one. The place of baptism clearly carried symbolic force:

Sent. This man was sent by Jesus as Jesus had been sent by God (9:4). His sending anticipated the later sending of the apostles (20:21). The one who received light/sight immediately began his mission by giving fearless testimony to the enemies of the light (9:25–34). Throughout John, the image of sonship was linked to the image of being sent; to become a child of God was to be sent by him as a witness to his enemies.

To sum up: A man who had not sinned and whose parents had not sinned had been predestined to be sent as a witness to the light. His confession echoed the confession of many other believers: "One thing I do know, that though I was blind, now I see" (9:25). He completed his risky testimony to sinners; but they scoffed at him as one who had been "born entirely in sins." The work of God that Jesus had done was thus continued in the work of this beggar. The story points beyond the actors to the declarations of the Prologue and to the Genesis story of creation. This ultimate reference appears in the final words of the man whom Jesus "sent": "Never since the world began has it been heard that anyone opened the eyes of a person born blind. If this man were not from God, he could do nothing" (9:32–33). John used that word "never" not as a rhetorical hyperbole nor in the effort to heighten the miraculous but as a statement of fact. A necessary inference from this statement is that the blind man attributed his cure to a divine design before the world began and to a Son of Man who shared the creative power of God. The ultimate reference is to the Logos without whom "not one thing came into being" (1:3). One may paraphrase the second sentence thus: "If this man had not received his power from God he would not have had the power, by making mud, to create anything."

To interpret the truth of the story one needs to set it within those ultimate parameters, a world within which all the thought patterns made sense: the ideas of sin and punishment, of blindness and sight, of darkness and light. By thinking within that world, John's readers could distinguish those born of God from those born of God's archetypal enemy and could locate within the compass of specific human decisions the signs of new creation and of final judgment. "I came into this world for judgment, so that those who do not see may see, and that those who do see may become blind" (9:39; cf. 1:10). This declaration of intent shows that Jesus himself viewed blindness and sight as metaphors for sin and forgiveness, for damnation and salvation. This declaration also identifies his work as the work of God, which the whole episode was shaped to illustrate (9:3). The judgment of which Jesus spoke was God's judgment.

Such an understanding becomes clear when Jesus replied to the protest of the Pharisees: "If you were blind, you would not have sin. But now that you say 'We see,' your sin remains" (v. 41). An analysis of the poetic balance in this saying reveals the centrality of sin. The earlier antithesis of blindness/sight has become the antithesis of sin/forgiveness. He who was "the light of the world" was now serving as the judge of sin. Thus the basic concern of the whole chapter was not the miracle of healing a blind man but the greater miracle of judging sin in such a way as to reverse prevailing human judgments. The final condition of the self-assured Pharisees was this: "your sin remains." They were viewed as continuing in the inheritance of the sin of Cain, Adam, and Eve. Just as both the Prologue and the Genesis story of creation resonate within the identification of Jesus as the light of the world (and therefore the healer of blindness and the gracious forgiver of sin), so the story of Genesis 3—4 and the summary statement of John 1:10 resonate within this condemnation of *continuing* in sin. To remain in sin was to disclose one's commitment to the sin of the world and to the work of the devil (8:44).

I now extend the exploration into John 10, with its highly allegorical discussion of the shepherd and his own sheep. There is no sign of a shift in thought between these two chapters; time, place, and dramatis personae remain the same. The linkage in personnel is only implied, but it is real. Chapter 9 has a diverse set of actors: the blind man, his parents and friends, the disciples, Jews, Pharisees, and, at the center, God and Jesus, doing their works. Readers may find each of these present in the allegory: the gate, the sheepfold, the gatekeeper, strangers, thieves and bandits, hired hands and wolves, those who give death and those who receive life, a life that does not end. The allegory of the sheepfold is as crowded with actors as the dialogues of chapter 9. Just as the work of God in chapter 9 included the gift of sight to the blind by the Light of the world, so the work of the good shepherd in chapter 10 included feeding his sheep in a lush pasture, with its reminder of the good earth in Genesis 1.

Three times the sheep of this shepherd were called "his own" *(idioi)*. This use of the pronominal adjective links this allegory to the Prologue, which has this summary statement: "He came to his own [*idia,* a neuter] and his own [*idioi,* a masculine] did not accept him. But to all who received him, who believed in his name, he gave power to become children of God" (1:11–12, my trans.). Translators have often had difficulty explaining why this neuter becomes a masculine. The allegory of the good shepherd provides the reason. There the neuter is used because it modifies a neuter noun: sheep.

One can infer that John viewed the blind man as one of the sheep in the fold who received life from this shepherd in fulfillment of 1:11–12.

Later, John had occasion to use the same adjective to introduce a new division of the Gospel that focused on the care of the shepherd for his flock: "Having loved *his own* who were in the world he loved them to the end" (13:1). The character of that love is the underlying motif in the shepherd's prayer for these sheep. That prayer has a significant alteration: the "his own" of John becomes the "my own" of Jesus, and this "my own" becomes identical with the "your own" of God: "All mine are yours, and yours are mine" (17:10). This tight interdependence is contrasted to the ownership of those who reject the shepherd: "If you [the disciples] belonged to the world, the world would love you as *its own*" (15:19).

To complete the study, I look now at a verse in the Prologue that has long baffled interpreters. When John first introduced believers in Jesus as the children of God, he used a triple contrast: these children were born "not of blood or of the will of the flesh or of the will of man" (1:13). Why did he select these three negatives to clarify the birth and destiny of God's children? The previous analysis of the two families may open up new angles of interpretation.

What kind of begetting did John have in mind when he wrote that God's children were born "not of blood"? Because the noun is plural, a more literal translation would be: "not of *bloods*." Use of this plural *(haimata)* was as rare in Greek as it is in English. In fact, this is the only occurrence in the New Testament. On a few occasions it occurs in the Old Testament and Apocrypha, where the translators of the New Revised Standard Version have usually adopted the English "bloodshed" (Hos. 4:2; Nahum 3:1; Hab. 2:8, 12, 17; Sir. 22:24; 2 Macc. 14:18). Bloodshed connotes physical violence ending in death.

Reading John 1:5 with a knowledge of the entire Gospel, a knowledge that the narrator surely had, one may conclude that the attempts of the darkness to overcome the light of life referred, at least in part, to the attempts to kill Jesus, the Logos of God. Recalling the description of the other family in John 8, one can hardly avoid linking these two passages. Those who wanted to kill Jesus were children of the devil; that is, they were begotten of bloodshed. This murderer from the beginning had been responsible for all the blood that had been shed since Abel. By John's day that blood included the death of Jesus and of at least some of his messengers (16:1-3). All that bloodshed was a fulfillment of the curse on the serpent for his lies and violence:

Because you have done this,
cursed are you among all animals,
and among all wild creatures;
upon your belly you shall go,
and dust you shall eat
all the days of your life.
I will put enmity between you and the woman,
and between your offspring and hers;
he will strike your head,
and you will strike his heel.

(Gen. 3:14–15)

John viewed this curse as operating without a break from the death of Abel to the moment of writing. In that continuing conflict the serpent had often struck the heel of Eve's heirs and they had often struck his head. But in their birth God's children had now been freed from that curse. They had *not* been begotten of that endless cycle of violence; their birth had come prior to the serpent's initial lie, for God's *truth* had been instrumental in their beginning. So, too, their begetting had come prior to Eve's sin; God's *grace* had been instrumental in that birth (John 1:14–17). As a result God's children would never see the death predicted in the curse, though John was well aware of the martyrdom of Jesus and of his faithful messengers. Their life had its origins in the life of the Logos that was "in the beginning with God."

Looking at the second and third negations, one discovers that the syntax of the sentence separates them slightly from the first negation and binds the second and third together. The point here is hard to make clear in English without reference to the Greek, but this revision may help to make it a bit clearer: The children of God were begotten *neither* by the will of the flesh (the second negation) *nor* by the will of man (the third negation). The second and third negations are not identical yet they are somehow bound together by the *neither-nor (oude-oude)* and are distinct from the first negation. The three operative terms—will, flesh, man—are so general and vague that outside the context of the Gospel they can mean anything. They have specific meanings only within the context of the Gospel, and, more narrowly, the context of the Prologue. In that Prologue, this study has shown that the narrator was intent on giving a preview of the coming struggle between the two families and on showing that the outcome of that struggle had been assured by the Logos of God in the beginning. Accordingly, one has reason to raise the possibility that these two negations may have been intended to assert that God had lifted the second curse in Genesis, the curse on the first woman and the first man, and that God had forgiven both woman and man by the grace that had been present in the original design of God. Why should the narrator have chosen this second curse, of which the original recipient was the first woman? Possibly because in the Septuagint the Greek name for Eve was "life" *(zōē)* since she was "the mother of all living" (Gen. 3:20). The contrast in the Prologue may have been quite intentional. The curse had been lifted by the Logos of God in whom was life *(zōē)*, and this life was the light of humankind.

Genesis described that second curse with great care:

> To the woman [God] said,
> "I will greatly increase your pangs in childbearing;
> in pain you shall bring forth children,
> yet your desire shall be for your husband,
>   and he shall rule over you."   (3:16)

The first two lines asserted the agonies of a mother in childbirth. Although John, Paul, and the Apocalypse were familiar with this image (John 16:21; Rom. 8:22; Rev. 12:1ff.), that aspect of the curse was alien to the Prologue, perhaps because it referred to the time of birth rather than to the begetting, or perhaps because that aspect of the curse fell only on Eve's female descendants. By contrast, lines 3 and 4 applied to the role in begetting as played by both Eve and Adam and by both female and male descendants.

Lines 3 and 4 distinguish between two parts of a single curse, the woman's passion for her husband and a husband's domination of his wife. Together they form a dismal picture of marriage for which history provides altogether too much evidence. Many passages in both the Old and New Testaments assign comparable roles to husband and wife. It is worth asking, then, whether there was any resonance between the description of the curse in the two documents:

GENESIS: "your desire shall be for your husband"
JOHN: "the will of the flesh"
GENESIS: "he shall rule over you"
JOHN: "the will of man"

There is obviously little verbal identity, but there may be more similarity of meaning than first meets the eye.

For example, the Johannine term "will" may connote strong sexual passion, as in other early Christian documents (1 Cor. 7:37; 1 Tim. 5:11). Indeed, Louw and Nida, in their Greek-English lexicon, suggest as a translation of the Johannine phrase "sexual desires."[2] In some ancient texts, this passion on the part of women was traced to lures of the devil. The translation of the Johannine "the will of man" is also uncertain. Because *andros* is used, "the will of a husband" may be a preferable equivalent. If one accepts these two adaptations of the NRSV translation, the sexual passion of a wife for her husband and the desire of a husband to dominate his wife become congruent to the two elements in the Genesis curse. In this case, the Prologue distinguishes sharply between two families: the children begotten by God through his truth and grace, and the children begotten by Adam and Eve through the lies and hostility of the serpent.

The strongest support for this possibility is found in the First Epistle of John, which explicitly opposes "the will of God" to "the desire of the flesh": "all that is in the world—*the desire of the flesh*, the desire of the eyes, the pride in riches—comes not from the Father but from the world. And the world and its desire are passing away, but those who do *the will of God* live forever" (1 John 2:16–17). This contrast and the two births in the Prologue have a basic homogeneity of thought.

The Epistle has the same accent on the beginnings as the Gospel, not only in the opening verses but in the following chapters. In that beginning was "the word of life," a life in which believers share solidarity *(koinōnia)* with the Father and the Son. Those who receive the gift of that life can walk in the light of truth and escape the darkness that is the realm of lies. The Logos of God abides in all believers, whether fathers or children; for, unlike the world of John 1:10, they all *know* "him who is *from the beginning*" and they have all "conquered the evil one," the enemy of Genesis 3:15. Their sins have been forgiven, not as a matter of repeated individual gestures of forgiveness but as a matter of God's canceling the primal curse on all human lies and rebellions. If believers were to claim that they had been immune to such sin and such a curse, it would have been tantamount to lying, a proof that they had been born of the father of lies. That, in turn, would brand Jesus himself as a liar (1 John 1:8–10). By contrast, those who confessed their solidarity with sinners "from the beginning" received forgiveness through one whose death had become a sacrifice "for the sins of the whole world" (2:1–2).

Solidarity in the light was described in various ways: sharing in the Logos, in eternal life, in the Father and the Son. These various idioms were alternative ways of expressing their begetting as children of God (2:29; 3:9; 4:7; 5:1). All carried the same basic meaning as in the Prologue. "Those who have been born of God do not sin, because God's seed abides in them; they cannot sin, because they have been born of God. The children of God and the children of the devil are revealed in this way: all who do not do what is right are not from God, nor are those who do not love their brothers and sisters" (3:9–10). Cain appears as the prime example of devil begetting; he was a liar and murderer, an evildoer and brother hater. He did not have eternal life abiding in him (2:12–16). Jesus was the prime example of God begetting; instead of taking another's life he had given his own life, replacing the blood of Abel with the blood that "cleanses us from all sin" (1:7; 3:16). It was necessary to believe that Jesus Christ had come in the flesh, for otherwise humanity would have had no escape from the archetypal curse on "the desire of the flesh" (4:2; cf. John 1:14). Jesus' sacrifice had come after God's curse had produced its fatal legacy; otherwise the darkness would not have been overcome by the light. But the coming of that light, by way of that sacrifice, had represented the will of the one who had planned all things from the beginning and so had enabled those who confessed their sins to walk in the light of life. John 1:10–13 was the gospel writ small; 1 John was the gospel writ large.

Returning now to the problem of interpreting the three negations of John 1:13, I admit that it remains uncertain whether the narrator consciously referred to the Genesis curses in describing the second family. What is certain, however, is his double desire: to stress the significance of the birth of God's children through the grace of the Logos, and to contrast that birth to the birth of another family. Each family became visible through the doing of its father's will, through sharing in the works of that father. The unity of each family in this conjunction of wills is reflected in the three petitions of Jesus' prayer to his Father on the night of his arrest. He requested that his followers might become "one as we are one" (17:11, 21); that they might be made holy in the truth of God's word (17:17); and that they might be protected from the evil one, the devil (17:15). Those three petitions were interdependent, in that the fulfillment of each required the fulfillment of the other two. Such fulfillment would restore the glory and the love that existed before the world was created (17:5, 24), before that world was polluted by the devil, who had been a liar and a murderer from the beginning. In the name of Jesus, the evangelist thus gave the greatest possible importance to God's action in protecting his own children from the evil one.

By attributing such ultimate significance to membership in the two families, John by implication radically reduced the significance of other matters to which readers often attribute too much significance. Consider, for example, the endless discussions of the various titles used for Jesus in the Gospel. Within the scope of a single chapter (chap. 9) the narrative applies a wide range of terms to Jesus: "this man" (v. 29), "the man called Jesus" (v. 11), "rabbi" (v. 2), "a prophet" (v. 17), "the Messiah" (v. 22), "from God" (v. 33). The narrator appears to accept all these terms as true, rejecting only the term "sinner" (v. 24). But more important, none of them was considered necessary in the healing of the blind man; he needed only to obey the command and to accept his being "sent." It was the work of God that confirmed Jesus' action as justifying the titles "the light of the world" (v. 5) and "Son of Man" (v. 35). As Jesus himself made clear: to recognize the works of God was more important than to use the right title for Jesus (10:38); such works indicated that Jesus had come from God (9:33) as the pretemporal word of God: "Let there be light" (9:5; Gen. 1:3).

According to this narrator, the truth that Jesus had come from God and returned to God diminished the importance of human concern about both the how and the when of that advent and of that return. This Gospel does not have or need a birth story. "Where he was born" becomes a topic for discussion but is ultimately of little importance. So, too, the mystery of "where I am going" could not be understood in advance, even by his closest disciples (chap. 14); it was this *where* that became a dominant motif in the story of his appearances. The Gospel viewed the Passion as necessary; Jesus' commission would be fulfilled only when he was "lifted up from the earth." But the truth of his return to the Father, and his assurance that his disciples would be "where I am," tended to displace their confusion over the mode of his glorification. So faith itself, along with birth from above, came to depend on recognitions that Jesus had come from God and was going to God, both movements oriented around the reference to God's Logos through whom all things came into being (1:3). Because he had gone to the Father, his presence with them as Counselor-Advocate-Spirit enabled them to do even greater works than he had done. The unity of this family signified that the direct link between *there* and *here* diminished the importance of all other measurements of space and time.

In this same connection I may refer to the distinction that John recognized between Jesus' relation to his followers before his death and after his exaltation. They understood many things afterward that they had not understood before. He could do many things through them afterward that he could not do before. Some of the teachings given before his death may have been spoken by prophets after his death in his name. It is the legitimate work of historians to trace the differences in the human situation before and after his going to his Father. But the importance of those differences is small compared to the importance of being children of God, becoming one with Father and Son, and being protected from the evil one. Membership in that family was realized through the conjunction of divine choice ("You did not choose me but I chose you," 15:16) and human choice ("If you keep my commandments, you will abide in my love, just as I have kept my Father's commandments and abide in his love," 15:10). All values were measured by reference to that supreme value.

Consider some other values that were diminished by this yardstick. Degrees of economic prosperity or adversity seem to be ignored entirely, as are national security and independence. What Jesus said about peace applied to all the other gifts of grace: "I do not give to you as the world gives" (14:27). From the world followers could expect only social status and moral prestige comparable to that of their master (16:1–3). Descent from Abraham, with its heritage of racial, ethnic, and religious distinctions, provided no protection from the evil one. At the end of the Gospel, Jesus even denied any special virtue to disciples who were martyred in the line of duty as compared to those who did not suffer that kind of death (21:15–23). What was decisive was that same conjunction of divine election and the human will that became free by accepting it. Just as Jesus' food was to do the will of the one who had sent him, so, too, the food of his disciples was to respond loyally to his calling and his sending.

The Gospel of John thus makes clear the frontier between membership in the two families—to be born from above, to be baptized with water and the Spirit, to walk in the light, to be sent into the world on the same mission as the Master.[3] Other writings in the New Testament, however, are often more helpful in describing the modes of crossing that frontier. Accordingly, in the next chapter I examine some of those metaphors of transition.

Notes

1. Søren Kierkegaard, *Training in Christianity,* trans. W. Lowrie (Oxford: Oxford University Press, 1941), 200–02.

2. J. P. Louw and E. A. Nida, *Greek-English Lexicon of the New Testament* (New York: United Bible Societies, 1988), 1.292.

3. Since completing this chapter, I have extended my study of the Genesis connections of Johannine thought in two other essays: "The Promise of Life in the Gospel of John," *Theology Today* 49 (1993): 485-499; "Logos Affiliations in Johannine Thought", in R. F. Berkey and S. A. Edwards, eds., *Christology in Dialogue* (Cleveland: Pilgrim, 1993), 142–56.

5

From One Covenant to Another

Metaphors of Transition

That infinite change at which Christianity aims, whereby everything has in truth remained as it was and yet in an infinite sense has become new![1]

Various calendars give silent testimonies to their origins in religious societies. Jews, Christians, and Muslims begin their enumeration of the years at different points, events of continuing importance in the inception of those religions. Each religion measures historical developments from a distinctive starting point; each is reminded of this fact by the annual celebration of a new year of its own, each year receiving a new number replacing the old in sacred annals and each increasing the temporal distance from the moment of its creation.

The Christian calendar, which has become so completely secularized that it should probably be renamed the Western calendar, will soon mark a transition between the second and the third millennia. This fact has prompted a glut of analyses and forecasts. How should this present century and millennium be known and remembered? What should be the hopes and expectations for the next? The anticipated turning of the calendar page has raised the possibility of a turning in human fortunes. Will the new millennium mark a turning from the bloodiest period in history to a less warlike era? Can the millions of homeless and refugees look forward to surcease from the time of great suffering to a time of homecoming and homefinding? Can society move from famines in a world of competition to security in a world of interdependence? The nearness of a change in the calendar spawns forecasts of doom and dreams of dawn. Does the Christian gospel have any relevance to these obsessions?

One can have great sympathy with such fears and hopes without at the same time confusing them with those imbedded in the gospel. The world of thought in the New Testament confronts one with a different outlook in which the understanding of beginnings and endings is

103

remote from the current preoccupation with the operation of economic and political forces. One should not confuse with the popular
futurologies of this decade the primal and still normative biblical definitions of the old age and new or mistake the rites of passage between them. The apostles did not measure such matters by the
calendar.

A second source of current interest in this subject is the recent
emergence of a hodgepodge of New Age thinking and a plethora of
New Age cults, which give preference to the history of souls rather
than the history of international politics. Although of recent vintage,
these cults have already produced an encyclopedia that defines terms
and traces origins to spiritual roots in both the East and the West. An
overview of the movement offers this epitome: "This New Age Movement can be defined by its primal experience of transformation. New
Agers have either experienced or are diligently seeking a profound
personal transformation from an old, unacceptable life to a new, ex-
citing future."[2]

Some members prefer to think of this transformation not in religious but in spiritual terms; but the experience of inner change is
common to founders, leaders, and members. They describe their previous experience (the old age) variously: exploitation, illness, poverty,
boredom, purposelessness, hopelessness, slavery to the illusions of
power, the oppressive orthodoxies of social systems, economic as well
as religious. The life of these New Agers pulses with energy and vitality, a sense of abundance and excitement, a recaptured health and
hopefulness. The experience of transcendence is often so profound
that it is described as a rebirthing. The experience of being healed,
together with the doctrine of holistic health, is sometimes linked to
ecological activity for the healing of the earth. Diverse tools are used
to induce or encourage the transformation experience: meditation,
massage, tantric yoga, herbs, macrobiotic diets, astrology, use of crys-
tals, regular conversations with disembodied spirits through a channel, periodic transfers of spiritual energy from gurus to followers. The
power that brings the transformative experience is commonly assumed to emanate from a universal source of spiritual energy that
supports all existence and that goes by many different names, none
of which, however, is essential to it.

Important similarities exist between some segments of these cults
and the Christian movement of the first century, but there are also
salient contrasts. Cultists sometimes emphasize these contrasts as they
pride themselves on their emancipation from Christian orthodoxies
of all sorts. Of the similarities cultists are usually less aware, partly

because current forms of Christianity have not offered examples of the authentic newness of the gospel or of the actualities of rebirth.

I am tempted at this point to embark on an extensive analysis of these similarities and differences. Instead, I examine twelve texts from seven different documents to see how they visualize the contrast between the old age and the new and how they describe the modes of transition from one to the other. On the one hand, these soundings may better show the radical differences between the "new agers" of the first Christian generation and the more recent breed; on the other hand, they may also open channels of understanding between the two, channels that have long been closed to Christians, whether conservative or liberal, who have never themselves had any experience that could truly be called transformative.

Text One

John the Baptist appeared in the wilderness of Judea, proclaiming, "Repent, for the kingdom of heaven has come near. . . ." When he saw many Pharisees and Sadducees coming for baptism, he said to them, "You brood of vipers! Who warned you to flee from the wrath to come? Bear fruit worthy of repentance." (Matt. 3:1–8)

Matthew viewed John as God's spokesperson; his voice in the wilderness echoed the voice of Isaiah and therefore spoke with doubled authority. Many candidates for baptism volunteered, but none were more surprising than these religious leaders of Israel. To them, John's greeting was equally surprising—not a congenial greeting "Good morning, friends; welcome to our worship service," but a brusque and brutal accusation, "You children of snakes!" This was more than an insult framed to arouse fury; as a prophet he was telling them that this was their status in God's eyes. In the eyes of their fellows, they were religious teachers and priests, known and honored for their devotion to the law of Moses. But to God they were children of serpents, begotten of poisonous lies and deceit and betrayal. (Matthew 23:33 shows that vipers and serpents were classed together. The same Greek word for "serpent" was used in the Greek text of Gen. 3:15, with its fateful curse on the brood of the serpent, the first enemy of humanity.) Accordingly, John's greeting signaled the surfacing of the long enmity between these descendants of the serpent and the descendants of Eve and thus also the enmity that would lead to a final conflict in the crucifixion of Jesus.

This understanding of John's brutal welcome provides a clue to the answer to John's question: "Who warned you to flee?" The question called for an answer. Without knowing how the candidates for John's baptism answered it, one can be confident of John's implied answer. The warning had come from God, whose fiery wrath they were fleeing. God was also the answer Matthew and his readers would have given. Such flight was itself a confession of guilt, a confession of serpentine paternity, which John's question was designed to elicit.

Answering John's question in this way, one can comprehend what would be the fruit of repentance for these servants of Moses. Repentance would embody the recognition that their dignity as models of the righteousness of the law had been self-deception and that any self-assurance stemming from their Abrahamic legacy was equally false. If it was God who now warned them to flee from the fire (snakes were especially vulnerable to grass fires sweeping over the ground), if it was God's axe that was lying at the root of their tree, then repentance required them to jettison all thoughts of inherited or achieved superiority and security and to accept baptism into the coming age (vv. 11–12). By repentance they could participate in a kingdom within which the primal enmity between the serpent and God would be terminated; the parenthesis that had opened with the self-will of Adam and Eve and the murderous violence of Cain would be closed with this baptism of repentance. Thus listening intently to John's cry in the wilderness one detects a clue to the character of the two ages and to the narrow channel that marked the exit from one and the entrance to the other. That cry served to telescope all history into this confrontation between prophet and Pharisee.

Text Two

You serpents, you brood of vipers! How can you escape being sentenced to hell?   (Matt. 23:33, my trans.)

Like John, Jesus used this greeting in addressing a similar group, the authorized leaders of Israel. (This address seems to be telescoped into a period of instruction for his followers.) The polemical greeting of these "serpents" was followed immediately by a key question that should be taken seriously: "How can you escape?"

The question was placed at a dramatic moment in the Gospel narrative; these were among the last words Jesus addressed to these enemies before they succeeded in their conspiracy to kill him (26:4). Matthew had collected a series of woes, all forms of announcing God's final judgment. It was the prophet Jesus who was warning them, but his human warning conveyed God's hidden condemnation. Jesus also disclosed why that condemnation was correct: his adversaries were guilty of the very sins they condemned. They used their reverence for ancient prophets to hide from themselves their violence against current prophecy. They thus validated the truth that hypocrisy is "the only evil that walks invisible, except to God alone" (from John Milton's *Paradise Lost*).

But this sin was not limited to those respected authorities. All the murderers of prophets since Cain were members of a single generation whom God held responsible for "all the righteous blood shed *on earth*" (23:35). It was this generation that had been born as the brood of the serpent that had deceived Eve; they were the children of vipers indeed. Final proof of the charge would be offered within three days, when these very adversaries, after asking Pilate to release "a notorious prisoner, called Jesus Barabbas"(27:16), would cry out for the death of the innocent Jesus: "His blood be on us and on our children" (27:25). Matthew was, of course, writing this account after a number of Jesus' messengers had also been flogged and crucified.

Now one is ready to recognize the relevance of the question: "How can you escape being sentenced to hell?" Or is this perhaps more an exclamation than a question? As an exclamation it would effectively accent the impossibility that such hypocrites would recognize their inherited guilt and cease their violence. The momentum of fraternal hatreds had attained enough power to prevent such a sudden shaft of self-knowledge and such a complete reversal of behavior. "How impossible for you religious leaders to escape responsibility for this flow of blood!"

But one can and should read the same cry as a genuine question inviting a convincing answer. What could make such an escape possible? Escape required a miracle of honesty and a change of heart. Such a miracle might be accomplished if the murderers were loved by their victim, a love made possible in turn by God's grace and forgiveness. In that case, the children of the primeval serpent could escape being sentenced to hell. Such a miracle would mark the end of an age that began in Eden. A hint of that transformation occurs in the elegy that immediately followed the seven woes, an elegy in which God's own grief was expressed in the words of Jesus: "Jerusalem, Jerusalem, the city that kills the prophets. . . . How often have I desired to gather your children together as a hen gathers her brood under her wings" (23:37). Jesus' departure from the temple (24:1) signaled the climax in this conflict between the divine hen and her rebellious brood.

Text Three

The next text is a key declaration in a speech given by one of Jesus' apostles:

> By this Jesus, God has announced to you the forgiveness of all those
> sins from which you could not be freed by the law of Moses . . . a
> work of God that you will never believe.
>
>   (Acts 13:39–41, my trans.)

The occasion: A message on a Sabbath to a synagogue in Antioch of
Pisidia, after the congregation had listened to the law of Moses and
the Prophets.

The messenger: Paul, a Pharisaic persecutor of Jesus, who had received forgiveness from the very person he had been persecuting.

The message: "What God promised to our ancestors he has fulfilled
for us, their children, by raising Jesus" (vv. 32–33). Through him God
now announces forgiveness (v. 38).

This text implies that although obedience to the law of Moses may
bring forgiveness of some sins, there are many other sins for which
freedom requires "a work of God." To accept freedom from them is
to accept this "grace of God"; to reject it is "to judge yourselves to be
unworthy of eternal life" (v. 46). This contrast impels a reader to ask
two questions: What are these other sins from which forgiveness is offered? Why does that freedom convey the gift of eternal life?

The answer to the first question: the sins from which forgiveness is
not available through the law of Moses are those rebellions against the
creator by Eve, Adam, and Cain, as narrated in Genesis 3—4. Those
were human efforts to achieve independence from God by seeking
food, wisdom, and the beautiful in defiance of the will of the Creator
(Gen. 3:6). The penalties for those efforts were a continuing conflict
with the serpent, a cycle of violence between brothers, the agonies of
bearing children, the frustration of the marriage bond by passion and
domination, eviction from the garden, and exclusion from the tree of
life. The grace of God canceled these sins and thereby the penalties as
well. God offered this grace by raising Jesus from the dead, for in his
death were telescoped all those sins and penalties.

How did this resurrection mark the transition to eternal life for
those accepting God's grace? That act on God's part was a restoration
of creation to the situation described in Genesis 1, in which everything
was very good. The Creator had now opened the gate to the garden
with renewed access to the tree of life. The prophets (e.g., Isa. 49:6;
Acts 13:47) had promised this salvation, but the law had not made it
possible. This was the life rejected by the persecutors (Acts 13:27, 46).
The light of this new creation enabled all who accepted it to "bring salvation to the ends of the earth" (v. 47). The pattern of thought makes
forgiveness equivalent to freedom, to life, to light, to a share in the salvation of the earth, to an obligation to relay the good news.

Text Four

Then he began to teach them that the Son of Man must undergo great suffering, and be rejected by the elders, the chief priests, and the scribes, and be killed, and after three days rise again.

(Mark 8:31)

All the Gospels agree on this necessity, and virtually every writing in the New Testament makes this teaching an integral part of the good news. This verse in the earliest Gospel is indeed an epitome of the story of Jesus' struggle with the serpent, a struggle that began with the wilderness trial and ended with the climactic trial in the Gethsemane garden. Jesus' acceptance of suffering was the essential secret to his triumph in both trials.

From its inception the teaching has provoked incomprehension, mystification, misunderstanding, and various degrees of opposition and rejection among interpreters. Here I have only enough space to ask what most needs clarification in this text. Some points are obvious, such as the identity of the opposition and its fatal results. But among the most mystifying issues is the intended force of this tiny verb *dei* or "must." Who viewed the suffering as necessary and why did they so view it?

The enemies of the Son of Man were among those who considered his death necessary. Faithfulness to the law of Moses, which they felt obliged to defend, required them to punish this messianic claimant for his defiance of the law and for his blasphemy against God. They viewed his crucifixion as a necessary fulfillment of their own calling by God.

At first his followers had not accepted the necessity; they had even been the spokesmen of Satan in urging Jesus to adopt a less dangerous course (Mark 8:32). They had learned its necessity the hard way. Experience had taught them that their own repentance and forgiveness had required his death. Otherwise they would not have been freed from those sins from which the law had been unable to free them. Such necessity became a matter on which every apostle came, in time, to agree.

They, in turn, gave a united witness that Jesus himself had considered suffering, death, and resurrection as necessary to his mission. Moreover, they witnessed to the conviction that this necessity had represented the will of God. God was the source of the vocation and therefore of the *must*. Thus in this suffering God had enabled the apostles to discern the invisible struggle between God and Satan, between the Lord whom Jesus had obeyed and the lord whom the leaders of Israel had obeyed.

But why did God consider Jesus' rejection and his exaltation necessary? From the very first, various answers have been given. The course God had chosen was necessary

if Satan's success in deceiving the defenders of the law was to be disclosed, thus enabling them to recognize God's gift of grace;

if all the descendants of Adam and Eve, whether Jew or Gentile, were to be liberated from their share in the universal rebellion and curse;

if God's love for his enemies was to be demonstrated, so that the redemption promised in the Law and the Prophets might be realized;

if a final victory over the lies, deceits, and power of "the ancient serpent" was to be won for humanity;

if a new access to the garden and the tree of life was to be opened through a gift that no one could claim was earned.

Text Five

If any want to become my followers, let them deny themselves and take up their cross and follow me.   (Mark 8:34)

Immediately after describing the necessity laid on the Son of Man, Jesus declared that his followers were bound by this same necessity. Accordingly, the term "Son of Man" embraced a collective as well as an individual vocation. On this matter the Gospels again speak with a single voice, although they also make clear that it was not until after Jesus' resurrection that the disciples fully understood Jesus' teaching that the same necessity applied to their own vocation.

Before the events on Golgotha they had been an easy prey for the serpentine predator (Mark 8:33). Even on their last evening with Jesus they did not grasp the full force of his toast: "This cup that is poured out *for you* is the new covenant in my blood" (Luke 22:20). One of those who received that cup left the table to betray him. The arguments of the others over greatness disclosed their incomprehension of "the covenant in my blood." Peter deceived himself and tried to deceive Jesus with a false pledge. In short, Satan was able to "sift all of you like wheat" (v. 31). Contrary to Jesus' commands, they had secretly managed to carry purses and they had been ready to defend themselves with swords—exactly like the armed police who came to arrest Jesus. They amply proved themselves to be the transgressors for whom Jesus' intercession was necessary. He bore the sins of his closest companions and for them he poured out the blood of the new covenant (Luke 22:33–38). "The Son of Man must suffer." Two reasons for the "must," then, are that his death and resurrection were necessary for their forgiveness and for them to comprehend the vocational thrust of that covenant.

The meaning of the term "Son of Man" as used by and for Jesus has been an enigma for later interpreters; it has provoked endless and inconclusive debates. I think that these debates have been powerless to dissolve some fundamental convictions of the Gospel writers. First, the basic meaning of the term was provided by its identification with Jesus and therefore with the entire course of his ministry, from its inception to its continuation after his death. Second, the term conjured up reminders of the stories of creation and pointed to the similarity and contrast between Jesus as Son of Man and God's creation of Adam, the first man. Like Adam, Jesus was a firstborn son of God; unlike Adam, Jesus was a firstborn son whose death would offer rescue from the death of Adam and his descendants. Third, the term was a collective term in that "the new covenant in my blood" created a continuing solidarity in God's calling between this firstborn son and all his siblings.

Text Six

I have been crucified with Christ; and it is no longer I who live, but it is Christ who lives in me. And the life I now live in the flesh I live by faith in the Son of God, who loved me and gave himself for me.
(Gal. 2:19b–20)

Paul was clearly pointing back to a transition in his own story that was sufficiently violent to justify the brutal term "crucified," with its savage overtones of social shame, religious exclusion, violent death, and final futility. The transition was sufficiently complete to include the death of his former ego and the inception of a new self living under a new commander. Whereas earlier he had persecuted the church, trying to destroy it, Paul now invited the verdict of death and finally received it. The use of the term "crucified" was justified by the truth, as he testified in various places, that he had died to the law, to sin, to the flesh, to the world, and even to death. The records of his ministry support the truth of such assertions. Yet for all its brutality, the term "crucified" was no synonym for defeat or disaster; rather, it signaled a new creation (Gal. 6:14–15).

In Paul's own mind, this experience that he called crucifixion was far more than a shift from violent opposition to vigorous endorsement;

it was clearly an experience of inner reorientation so radical that it could be called rebirth. He had been crucified *with* Christ, *along with* Christ as partner in his crucifixion. "We are convinced that one has died for all; therefore all *have died*" (2 Cor. 5:14). It was at God's initiative that Christ had died for all and was now alive in Paul, who now lived by faith in the Son of God, "who loved me and gave himself for me" (Gal. 2:20; cf. 2 Cor. 5:15). The new creation was an action by which God had so bonded Paul to Christ that life in the flesh had become life in Christ.

Nowhere did Paul use this experience as a mark distinguishing him from other believers. If anything, it underscored his unfitness to be called an apostle (1 Cor. 15:9). His earlier behavior gave a special poignancy to his confession: "While we were enemies, we were reconciled to God through the death of his Son" (Rom. 5:10). Crucifixion was a mark establishing the solidarity of all believers, first as crucifiers and then as members of "the body of Christ." This mark made obsolete all inherited forms of measuring status, including the distinctions between Jew and Gentile, slave and master, male and female (Gal. 3:28). It was not a matter of personal tolerance or a social flexibility in overcoming racism or sexism or elitism. It was a matter of God's action in creating "a new humanity" freed from the "bondage to decay" and from a daily existence "subject to futility" (Rom. 8:20–21; all these images were echoes of Genesis).

Paul's experience and that of his siblings was proof that the fullness of time had come (Gal. 4:4–7), a time in which "nothing can separate us from the love of God in Christ Jesus our Lord" (Rom. 8:38–39).

Text Seven

The next text undescores the importance of the transition from one age to the other:

> It is impossible to restore again to repentance those who have once been enlightened . . . and then have fallen away, since on their own they are crucifying again the Son of God and are holding him up to contempt.   (Heb. 6:4–6)

Among Christian readers these verses have always aroused bewilderment and even vigorous rejection. These rejections grow out of a false reading of the passage that construes the author as saying flatly that there can be no forgiveness for any sins one commits after becoming a Christian. Such construal rests on two errors. The first error is that such an interpretation trivializes the act of falling away by identifying it with any infraction of the moral code that a church has made normative for its members. But this view ignores the type of situation faced by this author and his first readers. They belonged to a tiny ostracized and helpless community, some of whom were in prison, some were being tortured, and all were being tested by the prospect of death as a penalty for their faith in Christ (4:15; 10:32; 12:4). They could escape these hazards only by renouncing such faith. In this situation "to fall away" was to join those who, as descendants of Cain, crucified Christ and to repudiate "the new covenant . . . that speaks a better word than the blood of Abel" (12:24). It was to surrender the fearlessness by which the Messiah had destroyed the power of the devil (sure sign of the new age) and to confess one's slavery to the fear of death (sure sign of the old) (2:14–18). The issue was clear: to accept suffering with and for Christ or to join in crucifying him again—no trivial sin!

The second error is that such an interpretation trivializes the "enlightenment" by identifying it with almost any psychic afflatus an individual may have experienced in becoming a disciple. But in this epistle, this enlightenment is nothing less than sharing in the act of God in Genesis 1 when by his imperious command he first separated light from darkness. The citation given above omits several equivalent expressions for such enlightenment. Consider these assurances: Believers have "shared in the Holy Spirit," that *pneuma* that had first "swept over the face of the waters" (Gen. 1:2). They have tasted "the goodness of the word of God," the word that had brought all things into existence and had called everything good. They have tasted "the powers of the age to come" (cf. the language in Heb. 12:18–24). In short, they have crossed the boundaries from the old age into the new.

For them to turn back across those boundaries would be comparable to Peter's replying to the high priest after his arrest, "We must obey you rather than God" (cf. Acts 5:29), by Stephen's doing whatever was necessary to avoid being stoned (7:45–46), or by Paul's confessing to Felix that the charges against him were true (24:1–13).

All this is confirmed by the contrast between the two *earths*. One earth receives plenty of rain and produces an abundant crop for the farmer. This earth receives God's blessing. The other earth yields the farmer nothing but thorns and thistles. It is doomed to stand under God's curse. The first earth was the earth of Genesis 1 that God had called very good; the second was the earth of Genesis 3—4 that merited the curse. To hold fast to the hope or to fall away was to choose between life in the two earths (Heb. 6:7–8).

Text Eight

Be as crafty as serpents and as docile as doves.
                                        (Matt. 10:16, my trans.)

The biblical zoo displays many animals, few of which are more important than doves and snakes. This is a metaphorical zoo in which all animals call to mind human actions that have resembled animals or birds in key stories from the past.

This saying of Jesus has become a popular proverb, widely used by speakers with no connection to Jesus, addressing audiences who also have no connection. Jesus, its creator, has lost all control over its meanings—good reason to try to recover what kind of behavior he intended to signify by serpents and doves. The saying appears only in Matthew's Gospel, where it functions not as a clever proverb with universal relevance but as a command issued by Jesus when he sent out his carefully chosen disciples with a dangerous assignment. The hazards of that assignment prompted the command, which comes in the Gospel as part of a longer warning, a single sentence introduced by an exclamation that one can translate as "look" or "listen" or "watch out."

> On your guard! I am sending you out as sheep into the midst of wolves; you must become as crafty as serpents and as docile as doves.   (Matt. 10:16, my trans.)

The associations are clear: the doves are classed with the sheep, the serpents with wolves. The enmity of the wolves requires craftiness on the part of these sheep. The identity of the sheep is clear: these are messengers who deliver Jesus' gift of peace from town to town and from house to house. No less clear is the identity of the wolves: leaders of the synagogues who would flog the messengers and hand them over for trial, or angry enemies who would pursue them from town to town, or family members who would have them put to death. The messengers are on a kamikaze mission. The causes of this collision are also clear: the message of God's forgiveness, the healing of the sick, the exorcism of demons, the cleansing of lepers, the free gift of life to the dead—all those benefices offered by Jesus himself (10:7–8).

That anticipated collision explains Jesus' choice of serpents as the measure of craftiness. Genesis 3 had introduced the serpent as the most crafty of God's creatures, and the serpent had illustrated its craftiness in the successful deception of Eve. Because of the persecution by the wolves, a persecution that the sheep could avoid by reneging on their promises, these sheep need to be as crafty as the ancient serpent in order to survive. Jesus' craftiness had enabled him to survive the temptation in the wilderness as well as the temptation by Peter and to make the ultimate choice in the garden. He had outwitted this most dangerous predator and therefore knew the kind of craftiness his followers needed.

What of the docility, the innocence, the gentleness of doves? The dove first appears in the biblical zoo after the initial catastrophe had fallen on the sinful descendants of Adam, the flood, when God regretted the creation of people and animals and birds and "determined to make an end of all flesh" (Gen 6:13). After the floodwaters had receded, it was the dove, bringing back an olive branch (8:11), that proved to Noah that the crisis was over. The docility of the dove represented a message of peace, the very message being delivered by the apostles in Matthew 10. The dove was also the symbol of God's gift of the Spirit in baptism (Luke 3:22; Matt. 3:16). In his appearance before Caiaphas and Pilate, Jesus had exemplified both craftiness and docility and had provided a role model that his disciples would need when they continued his mission.

Text Nine

This is the message you have heard from the beginning, that we should love one another. We must not be like Cain, who was from the evil one and murdered his brother. (1 John 3:11–12)

A reader's expectations often determine what he or she hears in a given text; in this case such expectations often produce a vast distortion of the text's meaning. The moment one hears "we should love," one often discounts the significance of the injunction, regarding it as a conventional platitude used by a moral idealist in calling for a mild revision in daily behavior; thus Cain becomes an evil stereotype used as a rhetorical device to induce the desired behavior.

If one listens to this entire chapter, however, one discovers how wrong such an expectation can be. A first shock may be the discovery that hatred is seriously claimed to be nothing short of murder; all who hate others are, without exception, murderers (v. 15). Another shock comes with the realization that Cain serves as more than a horrible example: to hate as he did is to become a child of the devil; hatred determines one's family, one's residence, one's lineage direct and inescapable from "the evil one." Exactly like Eve, one has been duped (1 John 3:7). To hate is, in fact, a sin that from the beginning has been punished by death; the one who hates resides in the realm of death, excluded from life by the Creator. Hatred thus becomes a map of one's world, showing the extent and boundaries of the "old age."

Conversely, the act of love marks the entrance to another homeland, made possible by the Son of Man, who came to destroy the
works of the devil, "to take away the sins" that have resulted from the
devil's deception since the beginning. He provided the final measure
of love: "he laid down his life for us" (3:16). It was he who had
promised that those who love would become like him (3:2) and not
like Cain. To love is to live in him; the index of such love is to give up
lives for one another, though that means being hated by the world,
which is incapable of such love. Love becomes the only way of making the transition from death into life (3:14). To choose to love is to
disclose the presence of the God of love; that choice is the point of
migration from one age to the other. This is more than a conventional moral platitude; to this author it is a matter of salvation or
damnation.

When one interprets this epistle in such terms, the structure of
thought illustrates the four points of the biblical quadrilateral found
in 2 Esdras (see pages 4–6). Point one is the human experience of an
evil age that is inhabited by an evil generation, whose hatred, like
Cain's, discloses lineage as children of the ancient serpent. Point two
is the human experience of a new age and a new generation in which
the replacement of hatred by love signals an escape from death into
life. Point three comes into view when this gift of life is traced to the
prior strategy and action of God "from the beginning." The birth of
his children discloses his primal creation of light, life, and love, before the violence of Cain and before the serpent deceived Adam. The
fourth point is the miraculous manifestation of that beginning in the
"wonder" of descendants of Adam who give their lives for one another; such "mighty works" show that these lovers have been born of
the will of God and not of the will of the flesh or the will of a husband
(John 1:12–13). For God's children to give their lives for others is an
action that embodies all four points of God's strategy.

Text Ten

But you are a chosen race, a royal priesthood, a holy nation, God's
own people, in order that you may proclaim the mighty acts of him
who called you out of darkness into his marvelous light.

> Once you were not a people,
> but now you are God's people;
> once you had not received mercy,
> but now you have received mercy.
> (1 Peter 2:9–10)

This is a declaration not of independence but of a new creation and therefore of a new dependence. The origin of this people is traced to God's command in Genesis: "Let there be light" (Gen. 1:3). The new dependence is shown by the announcement that God's mercy has created this people out of nothing. The author thus traces the new age to an action on God's part that simultaneously marks the emergence of a new people and defines the boundaries of that community by the gift of unexpected, unmerited, and yet all-powerful mercy.

In his first chapter the author had indicated the emergence of this gift. The recipients had inherited "futile ways" from their ancestors (1:18, a faint but distinct echo from Gen. 3:17–19). They had been ransomed from those ways "by the precious blood of Christ, like that of a lamb without defect or blemish" (1:19, a strong echo of Israel's history of sacrifice, and a faint echo of the earliest lamb sacrifice, that of Abel, which had provoked his murder—Gen. 4:4–5). Christ's ransom had been God's intention even before Adam had sinned: Christ "was destined *before the foundation of the world,* but was revealed at the end of the ages for your sake. Through him you have come to trust in God" (1 Peter 1:20–21). Such trust marked the reliance of God's people on God's gift of forgiveness. God's Son had fulfilled Isaiah's promise, "He committed no sin, and no deceit was found in his mouth" (2:22; Isa. 53:9); Isaiah's promise, in turn, had recalled the deceit and the sin of the serpent and Eve. Throughout his crucial suffering, Christ had trusted in God's primal plan, and in carrying out that plan, "he bore our sins in his body on the cross" (1 Peter 2:24). Because this ransom had been God's plan from the beginning, the words "our sins" embraced all human bondage to sin from the beginning. Accordingly, the mercy granted to the newly created people of God freed them from the whole historical momentum of sin (2:23–24). God's flock had now returned to its original shepherd. Christ's death had the retroactive power even to include the liberation of all the sinners who had been held in prison since their rebellion at the time of Noah (3:18–20; Gen. 7:17–23). That same inclusiveness is symbolized by the announcement that all "angels, authorities and powers" had been made obedient to the enthroned Christ (1 Peter 3:22).

In marking the creation of a new people, Christ's death and exaltation marked the point where trust in God's mercy overcame the fear of God's justice, a deliverance that enabled members to conduct themselves honorably among the Gentiles as "newborn babes" who had been emancipated from deceit and malice, those primal sins described in Genesis. Whether persecuted by civil authorities, abused by brutal masters, or victimized by cruel husbands, they could now repay curses with blessings, because they had received God's blessing that had been assured to all who suffer for and with Christ. Their love, like his, now covered a multitude of sins (4:8). Sprinkled with his blood (1:2), they had been born anew through an imperishable seed, the creating word of God, a clear allusion to the creation of Adam in Genesis 1 and to the Christian gospel. According to the poetic imagination of John Milton, when the angel Michael told Adam of this consummation of God's plan, Adam replied:

> O goodness infinite, goodness immense,
> That all this good of evil shall produce,
> And evil turn to good, more wonderful
> Than that by which creation first brought forth
> Light out of darkness.[3]

Text Eleven

Blessed are the meek, for they will inherit the earth.

(Matt. 5:5)

To the casual reader, this declaration promises a very large reward, the earth, to a very small group of people, the meek. Such a promise is so incredible as to justify the charge that its author must have been subject to delusions. Yet without doubt he was totally sane. One must therefore examine his promise carefully, and the first step is to look at the context. That step may not at first help much, because the promise is anchored in a cycle of nine beatitudes, all of which are equally incredible. The meaning of each derives from the meaning of the entire cycle.

The historical author: Jesus, who gave the pledge to his future apostles from a strategic and highly symbolic mountain.

The ultimate author: the God who authorized this prophetic Messiah to issue such assurances.

The literary author: a Christian editor, teaching a Christian congregation after the Messiah's promises had been verified by his exaltation.

The first audience: a Christian congregation, who would be listening in worship both to the reader and to their exalted Lord, in a situation of crisis described in the last two beatitudes (5:10–12).

The focus of the promises: the nine blessings were expressed in various images, all of which described the covenant that God had sealed with this community: a king and his subjects; a judge and his suppliants; a peacemaker and his mediators; a supplier of food and the consumers; a hidden deity and seeing eyes; a crucified criminal and followers persecuted on his account; finally, the promise of the earth made by one meek man to his heirs.

The earth is a spatial image. Initially it conjures up in one's mind a huge map of all the continents and islands. The other eight images, however, immediately discourage that impulse, because they carry parallel meanings that are independent of spatial measurements. They focus one's thought, for example, on hungry people eating a meal, or on a judicial courtroom, or on gates through which refugees are reaching a haven, or on a home where children are being born, or on the recesses of the heart where persecution is being endured and purity is found. The meek are promised an earth where all these events are transpiring; which makes it impossible to measure *this* earth in acres or continents.

The effort to locate this earth profits from another context—Psalm 37, where a similar promise appears no fewer than six times (vv. 3, 9, 11, 22, 29, 34). Studying this psalm, one finds the thought oscillating between two extreme choices: between dwelling securely in the earth and withering in time of drought, between having abundance in a day of famine and vanishing like smoke, between receiving God's blessing and being cut off by God's curse. This earth, of which the psalmist speaks, offered no place for oppressors but security and permanence for all who trusted in the Lord. The earth promised to the meek is the work of the Creator who, in creating it, pronounced it to be very good. It is significant that this psalm from which Jesus' beatitude was a direct quotation (37:11) is resonant with the imagery of Genesis. Like the psalm Jesus' blessing announced the end of God's curse and the reinstatement of God's blessing. Earth has become the place where sins are forgiven and food is abundant in the midst of famine. To inherit *this* earth is a blessing that conforms closely to the eight other beatitudes. Readers of Matthew need an imagination capable of coping with all these promises simultaneously. To import into such promises a literal conception of the earth as a vast extension of linear space is to guarantee a misunderstanding of this kind of language and thought.

Once one has located the earth on this invisible map, it is not difficult to recover the qualifications of the meek, for this meekness must conform to the character of the other recipients of God's kingdom and members of his family: the poor in spirit, the pure in heart, those famished for righteousness, those who forgive their persecutors. Each image throws light on the others. The recipients of all nine blessings are the meek; it is they who receive the promise of the earth, the good

earth of Genesis 1. Of this composite meekness, Jesus was the complete exemplar (Matt. 11:25–30; 21:5). His fulfillment of God's demands had qualified him to relay these promises to his siblings from
the mountain of revelation. The antithesis of such meekness had been
the serpent and his dupes, who had been evicted from the good earth.

Such an interpretation of the text avoids many perverse interpretations of the biblical perceptions of space and time. One of the most
destructive of these interpretations has been traced to Archbishop
James Usher, who first conceived the idea of dating the act of creation
at 4004 B.C. Such reliance on dates absolutizes temporal calculations
in a way antithetical to the sense of time inherent in either Genesis or
Matthew. A second demonic interpretation may be traced to those
who first located the boundary between heaven and earth at the moment of a person's death, at the customs barrier where Saint Peter is
supposed to stand, examining the credentials of dead souls, one after
the other. Such a conception destroys biblical perceptions of both
space and time. No less perverse is an interpretation that identifies the
earth that Jesus promised to the meek with a cartographer's drawing.
That view reduces the promise to the fantasy of an imbecile. The fulfillment of the promise remains miraculous, but its credibility depends
on whether this God of grace does, in fact, bless his human children
with the inheritance to which the nine images point.

Text Twelve

I translate this text freely, and in three segments, in order to exor-
cise demons of familiarity and to accent resonances that were indigenous to Matthean thinking. This is a prayer addressed to their Father
by those who have become his children through the mission of his
Son (5:43–48; 11:27; 12:50; 23:9).

> Our in-heaven Father:
> Let the holiness of your name become as fully honored
>   on earth as it is in heaven;
> Let the authority of your kingdom become as fully established
>   on earth as it is in heaven;
> Let the design of your will become as fully realized
>   on earth as it is in heaven.
>   (Matt. 6:9–10, my paraphrase)

In their praying, this family traced the origin of all things to the design of God. They celebrated family ties to this invisible Father, ties
that bridged the elusive distance between heaven and earth; the two

realms are distinguished, but the prayer calls for overcoming the distinctions. In Matthean thought, these first three petitions reflected at least four basic perceptions of how such a change takes place. (1) At an earlier time God's authority in heaven had been challenged by another invisible authority (4:1–11). (2) This Father had recently overcome that challenge, at least within the heavenly sphere. (3) His authority could now be extended to earth and, indeed, was even now being extended through Jesus as God's spokesman. (4) Such an extension had become the consuming desire of God's other children, whenever they uttered these same petitions for these changes on earth.

Each of these perceptions was supported elsewhere in the Gospel, though limited space here prevents more than a brief sampling of the evidence. The earlier challenge had been issued by the devil, beginning immediately after Jesus' baptism. That was the first of many subsequent occasions when Jesus had pointed to the defeat of Satan in heaven—when he announced the forgiveness of sins (Matt. 9:6), when he evicted demons (12:28), when he gave similar authority to his messengers (10:1; 16:19; 18:18), and when he repelled the devil's final tests in Gethsemane. Each exercise of his authority on earth was evidence that God's authority, effective in driving the adversary from heaven, was being extended to earth (Luke 10:18; Rev. 12:10–12). Whenever members of God's family used these petitions, they themselves became the *area* where this same authority was being extended even further in the creation of a new earth. Through its praying the church was both hailing the new age and exhibiting its arrival.

The first three petitions led simply and logically to the next two, answers to which serve as further exhibits:

> Today, give us our _____ bread,
> And cancel our debts as we cancel others' debts to us.
> (6:11–12, my trans.)

The first of these requests has perhaps suffered the greatest erosion in force through ceaseless repetition over the centuries. Although almost everyone now assumes that its meaning is entirely obvious, its precise meaning is almost impossible to verify. To identify the central problem I have used a dash to indicate the adjective that modifies the noun "bread." That Greek adjective *epiousion* appears nowhere else in any documents that would help to determine its meaning in this text. As a result no translator can be sure of its meaning here. Scholars get some help by analyzing the construction of the word, but their best efforts do not eliminate a large margin of uncertainty. Every written translation should therefore append a footnote to the word "daily": "the meaning of the Greek is uncertain."

Accordingly, it is necessary for interpreters to seek help both from the immediate literary context and from the thought world that gave the prayer its original reason for being. This is the prayer of an earthly family dependent for earthly sustenance on the gift of bread from their heavenly Father. In this connection, the following observations become germane. The bread that this family needs enables them to fulfill their assignment from this heavenly Parent—surely not the kind of bread that an accursed Adam (or his descendants) wrested from the thorns and thistles of an accursed earth (Gen. 3:17–19). In scripture the nearest analogy to a gift of heavenly bread was the manna provided to Israel in the wilderness during the "forty years, until they came to a habitable land" (Ex. 16:35). Each morning, as a result of Israel's need and in response to their complaining, God sent manna from heaven to the earth so that "those who gathered much had nothing over, and those who gathered little had no shortage" (16:18). God attached to each gift of this food the stipulation that it must be consumed daily and not be stored overnight (16:19). If one translates the Greek word *epiousion* by the English "daily," it may allude to this gift from heaven, possibly under the influence of the Exodus phrase "the bread *of* the day *for* the day" (*to tēs hēmeras eis hēmeran*, 16:4–5 LXX).

No doubt some early Christians linked the gift of God to the heavenly manna. The prophet John promised to faithful disciples "the hidden manna," food "from the tree of life" (Rev. 2:7, 17). The Gospel of John, in using the prayer "Give us this bread always," defined this bread in highly symbolic terms as the bread that does not perish but "endures for eternal life" (John 6:27). Those who eat this heavenly food will never grow hungry (6:33–35) and will never die (6:50). When they eat Jesus' flesh, they will receive Jesus himself into their flesh as the true "bread of life." The Greek word *epiousion* may be so rare precisely because it alludes to this rare bond between heavenly gift and earthly response. "Today give us this hidden manna." "Today give us this fruit from the tree of life." "Today give us this bread of life."

Three features in the manna tradition may resonate within this petition in the Lord's Prayer. First, the food is explicitly labeled the grain of heaven, the bread of angels, and bread from heaven (Ps. 78:24; 2 Esd. 1:19). Second, it was by this food that God sustained his people during the forty years of their wilderness sojourn (Neh. 9:20), ceasing this help as soon as the tribes reached their destination (Josh. 5:12). Third, Moses clarified God's intention in dispensing this aid: it was designed to humble and to test the pilgrims and to demonstrate to them that "one does not live by bread alone, but by every word that comes from the mouth of the LORD" (Deut. 8:3; see v. 16). This was exactly the "word" to which Jesus appealed in the wilderness when he was able to repel the first temptation—how appropriate to fashion his disciples' petition to recall that first great triumph![4]

Such a reading of this fourth petition links it closely to the first three, with their "on earth as in heaven," and also to the following petition. This need for forgiveness proves the kinship of this family with Adam and Eve, so that the fulfillment of the prayer restores the divine-human bond to the condition in Eden before their fall. In breaking the earth's slavery to sin, the divine answer fulfills on earth the original design when God gave earth his blessing: "very good." Moreover, because this petition made God's forgiveness of his people dependent on their forgiveness of their enemies, a positive answer restores the condition of humanity to the time before the archetypal instance of fratricide.

The final two petitions continue the same line of thought within the same linguistic universe.

> Don't subject us to the time of testing,
> but (if you do) rescue us from the evil one.
> (Matt. 6:12, my trans.)

Matthew's story of Jesus indicated how much his disciples needed this kind of help. He had been subjected to the greatest conceivable tests: in the wilderness, during his teaching of disciples and his response to enemies, in his never-ending battle with demons, in the garden, on the cross. His followers, testifying to his heavenly enthronement after his death, faced similar times of testing set by the same enemy (e.g., 5:10–12; 10:16–25). When these final petitions are taken seriously, they become a transcript of an inner struggle that determines which of the two competing lords would win the obedience of those who were praying. Only if the first three petitions in the series were answered could these final petitions be realized. When these final petitions were answered, the first petitions would be realized. Thus the entire prayer has a coherence that helps to define the meaning of each petition.

To understand this prayer in these terms requires the restoration of three contexts faced by Matthew's readers: their testing by severe persecution, their faith in Jesus' victory over the evil one, their memories of the good earth of Genesis 1 before the serpent's successful lies. By their quiet, unostentatious use of this family prayer, a Christian congregation both verified the transfer of authority from one lord to another and were themselves welcomed into the renewed earth. All this would be true, of course, only if God answered their prayer.

Jesus' final words to his disciples gave them an assurance of such an answer. He had now been given authority over both heaven and earth (28:18); they could therefore trust his power to answer their petitions. "Let the design of your will become as fully realized on earth as it is in heaven."

A Return to the Beginning

I began this chapter with a reminder of the popularity of current preparations for the calendar shift from one millennium to the next. An innate human impulse seems to demand an effort to synchronize human fortunes with chronological charts, as if the year 2000 were more significant than 1922 or 2011. None of the texts examined has encouraged such a tendency, and in this respect they represent scripture as a whole. Such lack of interest in dates has made it impossible for later generations to recover even the precise date of Jesus' birth or death. To be sure, early chroniclers assigned some events to the reign of a Jewish governor or a Roman emperor, but they measured the beginnings and endings of an age, whether old or new, within different horizons. Today, before people say "age" they have already thought of specific dates, but before early Christians said "age" they had already thought of God's plans and intentions. It was through God's creativity that an age dawned or was terminated. Accordingly, the apostles measured time by the vocation of God's people—its inception, course, and consummation—not by solar or lunar calendars. To say this is not to discount the depth and power of modern hopes that a new millennium may bring a transformed prospect; it is simply to observe that for the apostles the fulfillment of the deepest human hopes was not subject to correlation with the calendar, whether Greek or Jewish or Christian. Just as the modern penchant reflects an assumption that the play of political and economic forces determines human destinies, so the apostles assumed that the will of the Creator was decisive and that his will had foreknown the end from the beginning.

I began this chapter also with a brief glance at the recrudescence in recent years of a congeries of New Age cults with their hunger for "a primal experience of transformation." This case may seem to have a greater affinity with the apostolic writings, since in both movements one hears fervent summaries of the experience of a rebirth that is independent of those dates that historians use to carve history at the joints. Early Christians were as insistent as these New Agers on the

radical difference between the old age and the new and on the need
to migrate from one to the other. But it would be a mistake to discern
any generic kinship either of outlook or of inscape. The apostles
fixed on the first two chapters of Genesis as a prototype of God's creation and on the next two chapters as recounting the beginning of
the old age. They traced the inception of the new age to a design of
God "before the foundation of the world." This design had been revealed to them through the vocation of God's firstborn Son, the second and last Adam, the Son of Man, who had opened the way to
migration out of the old age. The more clearly the apostles defined
the two ages and the transition between them, the more distant becomes their world of language, thought, and experience from the
world of New Agers, who seek psychic transformation through chan-
neling, tantric yoga, spiritual aerobics, astrology, herbal diets, or the
transfer of spiritual energy from Eastern gurus to Western novitiates.
One gains little by forcing some kind of conceptual or experiential
synthesis between the biblical apostles and these gurus.

Students must sooner or later recognize the uniqueness of the apostolic thought world. One does not dispel this uniqueness by comparing
that world with other perspectives that might increase its intelligibility
or make it more amenable to assimilation into modern worldviews. It is
more profitable to ask this question: *Why* did early Christian authors
refer so frequently to the Genesis stories of Creation and Fall, whether
by explicit quotation, conscious allusion, or less conscious resonance?
One can give various answers to that question. Perhaps these references function as a strategy for using scripture to buttress the authority
or wisdom of the apostolic authors. Investigation may unearth isolated
instances where this explanation is sufficient, but it is far from persuasive in the case of Luke-Acts, 1 Corinthians, the Gospel of John, or the
twelve texts examined in this chapter. The authority of those authors
did not depend on their dexterity in marshaling scriptural quotations
in their support. Or perhaps they appealed to the Genesis traditions as
a rhetorical device to trigger an emotional experience of rebirth on the
part of scripture-obsessed readers, thus seeking as experts to tap into
spiritual energy for the sake of credulous amateurs, like modern tele-
vangelists. Even less evidence supports this explanation. Or did the
apostles appeal to the scriptures as an aid in persuading reluctant followers to endorse a body of orthodox doctrines or archaic codes of behavior? Instances of such use may be found, but they are far less
frequent and less typical than one might expect.

Only one explanation of the complex, many-faceted linkage between Genesis and apostolic thought is adequate. Along with many

other books of scripture, such as the Psalms and Isaiah, the language of Genesis had become the native language of Christians. It stocked their store of images and idioms that gave shape, color, and substance to their thinking about "the times of the Most High." Apostles felt completely at home in the symbolic world that had earlier found expression in scriptural stories, songs, and prayers. They were longtime residents in the world of God's creation, of serpentine lies and trickery, of the first Adam and the last. That is why in their allusions to Genesis they seldom used quotation marks; thinkers seldom use such marks when they are thinking and speaking in their native tongue. Indeed, scripture becomes scripture only when it quietly defines the boundaries of the world in which a community lives and when it supplies the language with which that community thinks. One can find traces in the New Testament of influences from non-Jewish sources, but the decisive metaphors for articulating the transition from old age to new were drawn from the rich scriptural lexicon, metaphors like forgiveness, atonement, ransom, adoption, liberation, rescue, peace.

Just as any language demonstrates its vitality by an interaction between the linguistic legacy and the current situation, so scripture comes alive as scripture when it provides a convincing context for thinking about new situations. One should detect in this homogeneity between inherited language and emerging life the primary clues as to what it is that imparts authority to scripture as scripture. A body of writings becomes truly sacred when it creates an imagined world where a community feels most fully at home and where the Holy Spirit speaks most powerfully to the spirit of the community. Terms like "authority," "power," "scripture," and "holiness," derive their meaning and force from the mysterious and largely subconscious communal recognitions that life makes sense within this imagined universe. The God who is truly a community's deity speaks to it most profoundly within the borders of this spiritual homeland. The Old Testament has remained sacred to the Christian community for many reasons, but this is one of the most basic and enduring: this scripture continues to release the most profound resonances between the imagined world of God and the daily struggles of God's people. It continues to furnish the essential metaphors for creation and damnation, blessing and curse, birth and death; such metaphors give shape and direction to all human stories.

This profound linkage between new experiences and the inherited language, however, always opens the way for a changed understanding of that inheritance. Those who were called through God's primal word discovered that their former language shared in the rebirth.

When they read Moses in the light of the new covenant in Jesus' blood, they discovered new implications in all the earlier covenants—those with Moses, Abraham, Noah, and Adam. Examining Romans 5—8, for example, one may see not only how Paul's understanding of the sin of Adam influenced his understanding of God's love in Christ but also how the experience of the love of Christ influenced his reading of Genesis 3. Having been reconciled to God by the death of God's Son, Paul recognized in this man's act of obedience power to overcome the catastrophic effects of Adam's disobedience (Rom. 5:18–21). His understanding of Adam's death in sin had been transformed by his understanding of the death of Christ to sin, by which sin's dominion had been broken. Thus Paul traced universal redemption to the creative design of God before the creation of Adam. Children of God had been born by the Spirit into a larger family, a birth in which each child had been "predestined to be conformed to the image" of God's firstborn Son—a most radical reinterpretation of Genesis 1 (Rom. 8:28–30).

The Epistle to the Hebrews is filled with other examples of how the old language was renewed, the fulfillment of scripture inducing revisions of scripture. Christ is the one through whom God created the world (1:2); accordingly, it is to Christ that the coming world is subjected (2:5). It had been through death that the devil had established his power; accordingly, it was through Christ's "death for everyone" that he had freed the slaves of the devil (2:9, 14). The Creator had created the Sabbath as a time of rest; that rest now became both a promise and a goal for the obedient, with exclusion a supreme penalty for the disobedient (4:1–11). The blood of Abel had spoken one word; the sprinkled blood of Jesus spoke a better word (12:24). Between the stories of Abel and Christ a magnetic field was thus established, each story resonating to the other and helping to interpret the other.

The apostolic reinterpretations of scripture were so extensive that few of the previously authorized interpreters of those covenants could accept them. Those reinterpretations produced a Christian Old Testament that is different from the Hebrew scripture, notwithstanding almost complete identities in canon and text. Christian and Jewish scholars do not often contest the verbal content of Genesis 1—3, but they do have radical disjunctions in interpretation. These disjunctions had their historical origins in vigorous debates between Jesus and the scribal leaders of Judaism; this conflict is reflected in the repeated announcements, "the Son of Man must undergo great suffering." That suffering, in turn, evoked many of the greatest alterations in Christian understandings of scripture. The postcanonical history of the two religions has certainly shown that conflicts over the interpretation of Genesis 1—3 have been virtually inescapable as well as insoluble. In those conflicts both Jews and Christians have vindicated their loyalty to their respective vocations; the conflicts disappear only when that loyalty evaporates.

Of the deadlock between the two interpretations of scripture no one was more keenly aware than Paul. It had been his vocation as a Pharisee to persecute Jesus (Acts 9:5). His vocation as a messenger of Christ induced him to accept persecution from his former colleagues. In both callings he considered himself loyal to the same God "from whom and through whom and to whom are all things" (Rom. 11:36). Loyal to the scripture before his calling from Christ, he considered himself even more loyal afterward. He believed that the gospel was a fulfillment of scripture that disclosed new meanings in that scripture, including the stories of Creation and Fall. But the more loyal he was to the new Master, the more bitter the hostility of his former colleagues over his reading of scripture.

This is not the place, however, to explore further that deadlock.[5] It is in order, however, to remind Christians today that their loyalty to the covenant in Christ's blood demands more than partisan wrangling. In revealing God's love for his enemies, that covenant demands such love on the part of his children. In this they have Paul's own encouragement: "I could wish that I myself were accursed and cut off from Christ for the sake of my own people" (Rom. 9:3). In marking the boundary between Christianity and Judaism, the new covenant goes even further. It locates the beginning of the old age long before the separation between Judaism and Christianity in the cycle of lies, deceptions, and acts of violence from which the covenant with Moses had proved unable to free all the children of Adam and Eve. In the new age God restored the bonds to his creation that had been cut long before the emergence of any religious bodies, including the Christian.

Today it is Christian leaders who hold positions comparable to those once held by the Pharisees and who therefore are threatened by similar self-deceptions. It is they who need to recall how Jesus identified the Cain generation: those who build impressive memorials to God's ancient messengers and who say, "If we had lived in the days of our ancestors, we would not have taken part with them in shedding the blood of the prophets" (Matt. 23:30). All such forms of pretension and self-deception are destroyed by Christ. As certainly as he once breached the walls between the righteous and the sinners, or between Jews and Gentiles, he continues to demolish the walls that

Christians erect between themselves and others. The covenant in Christ's blood is no less destructive of such walls than when he shed that blood. By the same token, however, when the word of God again summons light out of darkness, it is no less liberating; it enables members of all religions or of none to have access again to the tree of life.

This study of early Christian visions of a new creation illustrates a truth that George Lindbeck applies to modern Christian experience: "Just as an individual becomes human by learning a language, so he or she begins to become a new creation through hearing and interiorizing the language that speaks of Christ."[6]

I close this journey of exploration into the basic language of the Christian community by expressing two convictions. First, the Old Covenant will never become fully our own unless and until we understand the Genesis story of creation in such a way that the episode of the serpent's lie is heard again by the heirs of Adam with all its original, universal, sinister overtones. Second, the New Covenant will not become fully our own unless and until we hear the good news of Jesus in such a way that it liberates us from satanic deceptions and Adamic rebellions and until through that liberation we gain a new understanding of God's design for our own work. A former Pharisee summarized that design succinctly in an appeal to Christians in Rome: "In the first Adam God imprisoned all in disobedience, both Jews and Gentiles, so that in the last Adam he might be merciful to all, both Jews and Gentiles" (Rom. 11:32, my paraphrase).

Notes

1. Søren Kierkegaard, *Works of Love*, trans. David F. Swenson and Lillian M. Swenson (Princeton, N.J.: Princeton University Press, 1946), 110.

2. J. G. Melton, *New Age Encyclopedia* (Detroit: Gale Research, Inc., 1990), xiii.

3. John Milton, *Paradise Lost* (New York: New American Library, 1961), 12.469–73.

4. This emphasis in the prayer on the divine source of the bread confirms my use in earlier chapters of this book of the adjective *before*. The family of this Father is sustained every day by relying on the gift of prevenient grace, on bread that comes "from the mouth of the Lord."

5. My separate essay, "Blasphemy Backdated," *Horizons in Biblical Theology*, 1993, 15: 38–51.

6. George Lindbeck, *The Nature of Doctrine* (Philadelphia, Westminster Press, 1984), 62.

Selected Writings of Paul Sevier Minear

Compiled by
Richard H. Minear

I. Books

An Introduction to Paul. Nashville: Abingdon, 1937.

And Great Shall Be Your Reward: The Origins of Christian Views of Salvation. New Haven: Yale University Press, 1941.

Eyes of Faith: A Study in the Biblical Perspective. Philadelphia: Westminster, 1946. Rev. ed. St. Louis: Bethany, 1966.

The Choice. Philadelphia: Westminster, 1948.

The Kingdom and the Power: An Exposition of the New Testament Gospel. Philadelphia: Westminster; London: Lutterworth, 1950.

Kierkegaard and the Bible: An Index. With Paul Morimoto. Princeton, N.J.: Princeton Seminary, 1953.

Christian Hope and the Second Coming. Philadelphia: Westminster, 1954.

Jesus and His People. World Christian Books. New York: Association Press, 1956. Several translations.

Horizons of Christian Community. St. Louis: Bethany, 1959.

Images of the Church in the New Testament. Philadelphia: Westminster, 1960; London: Lutterworth, 1961. Paperback: Philadelphia, Westminster, 1970. Translations: German, Chinese, Japanese.

The Gospel According to Mark. The Layman's Bible Commentary. Richmond: John Knox, 1962; London: SCM, 1963. Translation: Japanese.

I Saw a New Earth: An Introduction to the Visions of the Apocalypse. Washington, D.C.: Corpus, 1968.

The Obedience of Faith: The Purposes of Paul in the Epistle to the Romans. London: SCM, 1971.

Commands of Christ. Nashville: Abingdon; Edinburgh: St. Andrews, 1972.

I Pledge Allegiance: Patriotism and the Bible. Philadelphia: Geneva, 1975.

To Heal and to Reveal: The Prophetic Vocation according to St. Luke. New York: Seabury, 1976.

To Die and to Live: Christ's Resurrection and Christian Vocation. New York: Seabury, 1977.

New Testament Apocalyptic. Nashville: Abingdon, 1981.

Pentecost 2. With H. B. Adams. Philadelphia: Fortress, 1981. Translation: Korean.

Matthew, the Teacher's Gospel. New York: Pilgrim, 1982; London: Darton, Longman & Todd, 1984.

John, the Martyr's Gospel. New York: Pilgrim, 1984.

Death Set to Music: Masterpieces by Bach, Brahms, Penderecki and Bernstein. Atlanta: John Knox, 1987.

The God of the Gospels: A Theological Workbook. Atlanta: John Knox, 1988.

II. Essays in Symposia

"The Relevance of the Message for Our Day." In *Contemporary Thinking About Jesus,* edited by T. S. Kepler, 308–13. Nashville: Abingdon, 1942; Reprinted from *Journal of Bible and Religion* 10 (1942): 88–92.

"Paul the Apostle." In *The Interpreter's Bible,* edited by G. A. Buttrick et al., 7.200–213. Nashville: Abingdon, 1951.

"The Covenant and the Great Commission." In *Missions Under the Cross,* edited by N. Goodall, 64–80. London: Edinburgh House, 1953.

"Work and Vocation in Scripture." In *Work and Vocation,* edited by J. O. Nelson, 32–81. New York: Harper & Bros., 1954.

"Christian Eschatology and Historical Methodology." In *Neutestamentlichen Studien für Rudolf Bultmann,* edited by W. Eltester, 15–23. Berlin: A. Töpelmann, 1957.

"Gratitude and Mission in the Epistle to the Romans." In *Basileia,* edited by J. Hermelink and H. J. Margull, 42–48. Stuttgart: Evangelische Missionsverlag, 1959.

"The Cosmology of the Apocalypse." In *Current Issues in New Testament Interpretation,* edited by W. Klassen and G. F. Snyder, 23–37. New York: Harper & Bros., 1962.

"The Meeting Place." In *Proceedings of the Ninth International Congregational Council,* 54–61. London: Independent, 1962.

"Thanksgiving as a Synthesis of the Temporal and the Eternal." In *A Kierkegaard Critique,* edited by H. A. Johnson and N. Thulstrup, 297–308. New York: Harper & Bros., 1962. Reprinted from *Anglican Theological Review* 38 (1956): 4–14.

"The Constitution on Revelation: A Protestant Appraisal." In *Vatican II: An Interfaith Approach,* edited by J. Miller, 68–88. Notre Dame, Ind.: University of Notre Dame, 1966.

"Rudolf Bultmann's Interpretation of New Testament Eschatology." In *The Theology of Rudolf Bultmann,* edited by C. W. Kegley, 65–82. New York: Harper & Row, 1966.

"Luke's Use of the Birth Stories." In *Studies in Luke-Acts*, edited by L. E. Keck and J. L. Martyn, 111–30. Nashville: Abingdon, 1966. Reprinted as *Das Lukas-Evangelium*, edited by G. Braumann, 204–35. Darmstadt: Wissenschaftliche Buchgesellschaft, 1974.

"The Church, Ecumenism, and Methodism." In *Methodism's Destiny in an Ecumenical Age*, edited by P. Minus, 19–43. Nashville: Abingdon, 1969.

"The Transcendence of God and Biblical Hermeneutics." In *Proceedings of the 23rd Annual Convention*, 1–19. Yonkers: Catholic Theological Society, 1969.

"Gospel History: Celebration or Reconstruction?" In *Jesus and Man's Hope*, edited by D. G. Miller, 2, 13–17. Pittsburgh: Pittsburgh Theological Seminary, 1970.

"Audience Criticism and Markan Ecclesiology." In *Neues Testament und Geschichte*, edited by H. Baltensweiler and B. Reicke, 79–89. Tübingen: J. C. B. Mohr, 1972.

"Communication and Community." In *New Theology No. 9*, edited by M. E. Marty and D. Peerman, 253–69. New York: Macmillan, 1972. Reprinted from *Theology Today* 27 (1970): 140–54.

"Heil in der Offenbarung des Johannes." In *Das Heil der Welt Heute*, edited by P. A. Potter, 83–93. Stuttgart: Kreuz, 1973.

"Barth's Commentary on Romans, 1922–1972." In *Footnotes to a Theology*, edited by M. Rumscheidt, 8–29. Supplement to *Studies in Religion*, Corporation for Publication of Academic Studies in Religion in Canada, 1974.

"The Disciples and the Crowds in the Gospel of Matthew." In *Gospel Studies in Honor of Sherman E. Johnson*, edited by M. H. Shepherd and E. C. Hobbs, 28–44. Supplementary Series, *Anglican Theological Review*, 1974.

"False Prophecy and Hypocrisy in the *Gospel of Matthew*." In *Neues Testament und Kirche*, edited by J. Blank and J. Gnilka, 76–93. Freiburg: Herder & Herder, 1974.

"J. S. Bach and J. A. Ernesti: A Case-Study in Exegetical and Theological Conflict." In *Our Common History as Christians*, edited by J. Deschner, L. T. Howe, and K. Penzel, 131–56. New York: Oxford University Press, 1975.

"Theology—Vocation or Profession?" In *Doing Theology Today*, edited by C. S. Song, 1–16. Madras: Christian Literature Society, 1976. Translated as "Rechenschaft über die Hoffnung als Berufung zur Theologie." In *Theologie im Entstehen*, edited by L. Vischer, 16–32. Munich: Chr. Kaiser, 1976.

"Unity, Pluralism and Mission." In *Festschrift for Lukas Vischer*, 40–55. Geneva: World Council of Churches, 1976.

"Leonard Bernstein, Theologian." In *Festschrift for Roger Hazelton*, edited by Charles E. Carlston. *Andover Newton Theological Quarterly* 17 (1977): 281–90.

"An Early Christian Theopoetic." In *Semeia 12: Fetschrift for Amos N. Wilder*, edited by W. A. Beardslee, 201–14. Missoula, Mont., Scholars Press, 1978.

"The Crucified World: The Enigma of Galatians 6:14." In *Theologia Crucis—Signum Crucis*, edited by G. Klein and C. Andresen, 395–407. Tübingen: J. C. B. Mohr, 1979.

"Faith and Freedom: A Case Study." In *Science, Faith, and Revelation*, edited by B. E. Patterson, 224–39. Nashville: Broadman, 1979.

"Some Pauline Thoughts on Dying." In *From Faith to Faith: Essays in Honor of Donald G. Miller*, edited by D. Y. Hadidian, 91–106. Pittsburgh: Pickwick, 1979.

"Ökumenischer Beitrag zur Pneumatologie." Translated by A. Berz. In *Unterwegs zur Einheit*, edited by J. R. Brantschen and P. Salvatico, 791–802. Freiburg: Herder, 1980.

"To Ask and to Receive." In *Intergerini Parietis Septum: Festschrift for Markus Barth*, edited by D. Y. Hadidian, 227–50. Pittsburgh: Pickwick, 1981.

"The Audience of the Fourth Evangelist." In *Interpreting the Gospels*, edited by J. L. Mays, 247–64. Philadelphia: Fortress, 1981. Reprinted from *Interpretation* 31 (1977): 339–54.

"Logos Ecclesiology in the Gospel of John." In *Christological Perspectives*, edited by R. F. Berkey and S. Edwards, 95–111. New York: Pilgrim, 1982.

"Diversity and Unity: A Johannine Case-Study." In *Die Mitte des Neuen Testaments*, edited by U. Luz and H. Weder, 162–75. Göttingen: Vandenhoeck & Ruprecht, 1983.

"My Peace I Give to You." In *Reformed Faith and Politics*, edited by R. Stone, 31–48. Washington, D.C.: The University Press of America, 1983.

"Rich Memories, Huge Debts." In *How Karl Barth Changed My Mind*, edited by D. K. McKim, 47–51. Grand Rapids: Eerdmans, 1986.

"The Peace of God: Conceptions of Peace in the New Testament." In *Celebrating Peace*, edited by L. S. Rouner, 118–34. Notre Dame, Ind.: University of Notre Dame Press, 1990.

"Singing and Suffering in Philippi." In *The Conversation Continues: Essays on Paul and John Presented to J. Louis Martyn*, edited by B. Gaventa and R. W. Fortna, 202–19. New York: Abingdon, 1990.

"The Death of Death." In *The Contribution of Carl Michalson to Modern Theology*, edited by H. O. Thompson, 245–58. Lewiston, N. Y.: Edwin Mellen, 1991.

"Inclusive Language and Biblical Authority." In *Faith and History: Essays in Honor of Paul W. Meyer*, edited by J. T. Carroll, C. H. Cosgrove, and E. E. Johnson, 335–51. Atlanta: Scholars Press, 1991.

"Propheten Gottes: Das Wesen ihrer Berufung." In *Ökumenisches Theologie in den Herausforderungen der Gegenwart*, edited by K. B. Gerschwiler, A. Karrer, C. Link, J. M. Lochman, and H. Rüegger, 175–91. Göttingen: Vandenhoeck & Ruprecht, 1991.

"Video and Audio in the Church." In *On Being the Church: Essays in Honour of John Snyder,* edited by P. Erb, 11–26. Waterloo: Conrad Press, 1992.

"Logos Affiliations in Johannine Thought." In *Christology in Dialogue,* edited by R. F. Berkey and S. Edwards, 142–56. Cleveland: Pilgrim, 1993.

III. Essays in Periodicals

"Current Issues in New Testament Studies." *Garrett Tower* 12 (1937): 1–6.

"Repentance." *Religion in Life* 7 (1938): 577–84.

"Morphology of a Proverb." *Anglican Theological Review* 21 (1939): 282–92.

"Historical Consciousness vs. Historical Knowledge." *Journal of Bible and Religion* 8 (1940): 72–76.

"The Resurrection of Jesus." *Religion in Life* 9 (1940): 174–81.

"How Objective Is Biblical Criticism?" *Journal of Bible and Religion* 9 (1941): 217–22.

"The Relevance of the Message for Our Day." *Journal of Bible and Religion* 10 (1942): 88–92.

"The Needle's Eye." *Journal of Biblical Literature* 61 (1942): 157–69.

"Concept of History in the Prophets and Jesus." *Journal of Bible and Religion* 11 (1943): 156–61.

"The Jerusalem Fund and Pauline Chronology." *Anglican Theological Review* 25 (1943): 389–96.

"Satan Returns from Holiday." *Religion in Life* 12 (1943): 187–96.

"The Biblical Sense of Community." *Journal of Religious Thought* 1 (1944): 77–96.

"Paul's Missionary Dynamic." *Andover Newton Quarterly* 36 (1944): 2–11.

"Time and the Kingdom." *Journal of Religion* 24 (1944): 77–88.

"Wanted: A Biblical Theology." *Theology Today* 1 (1944): 47–58.

"Form Criticism and Faith." *Religion in Life* 15 (1945): 46–56.

"Transmission of Faith through Biblical Forms of Communication." *Journal of Religious Thought* 4 (1947): 136–51.

"The New Testament Witness and Civilization." *Theology Today* 5 (1948): 340–49.

"Salvation." *Interpretation* 3 (1949): 259–72.

"The Interpreter and the Nativity Stories." *Theology Today* 7 (1950): 358–75. Also *Svensk Exegetische Årsbok* Supplement 13 (1950): 3–22. Privately reprinted, Washington, D.C., 1961.

"Between Two Worlds: Eschatology and History." *Interpretation* 5 (1951): 27–39.

"The Mystery of Baptism." *Religion in Life* 20 (1951): 225–35.

"The Time of Hope in the New Testament." *Scottish Journal of Theology* 6 (1953): 337–61.

"Christ, the Hope of the World." *Ecumenical Review* 6 (1953): 1–9.

"The Coming of the Son of Man." *Theology Today* 9 (1953): 489–93.

"The Meaning of Atonement in the Epistle to the Romans." *Interpretation* 7 (1953): 142–55.

"Adam and the Educator." *Christian Education* (South Africa) 12 (1953): 2–4. Reprinted in *Christian Scholar* 39 (1956): 6–18. Translated as "Adam und die Erzieher." In *Theologische Existenz Heute* 38, edited by K. G. Steck and G. Eichholz, 34–52. Munich: Chr. Kaiser, 1953.

"The Wounded Beast." *Journal of Biblical Literature* 72 (1953): 93–101.

"New Every Morning: A Study of 1 Peter." Bible Studies for Use at the Evanston Assembly, World Council of Churches, 1954.

"Revelation and the Knowledge of the Church" (The Dudleian Lecture). *Harvard Divinity School Bulletin* 20 (1954): 19–37.

"The World Council of Churches and the Churches Called Congregational." *Bulletin of the Congregational Library* (Boston) 5 (1954): 4–11.

"The Church, Militant or Triumphant?" *Andover Newton Quarterly* 47 (1955): 25–31.

"Ecumenical Conversations." A Guide for Commissions Preparing for the North American Conference on Faith and Order, National Council of Churches (1956).

"Who Seeks Church Unity?" *Christian Century* 73 (1956): 202–4.

"Thanksgiving as a Synthesis of the Temporal and the Eternal." *Anglican Theological Review* 38 (1956): 4–14.

"Action and Reaction in the Ecumenical Movement. *Religion in Life* 26 (1957): 163–68.

"The Significance of the Oberlin Conference." *Ecumenical Review* 10 (1958): 121–26.

"Images of the Church in the New Testament." *Southeast Asia Journal of Theology* 1 (1959): 7–12.

"The Structure of Church and Society in the Light of the New Testament." *Student World* 52 (1959): 17–24.

Editor, "Jesus Christ, the Light of the World." *Bible Studies for the New Delhi Assembly*, World Council of Churches, (1961): 7–31.

"Catholicity in Practice." *Ecumenical Review* 15 (1962): 39–44.

"He Is Our Peace," Bible studies prepared for the Annual Week of Prayer for Christian Unity. With Lukas Vischer. *Commission on Faith and Order* (Geneva), (1962): 3–34.

"The Peril of Modernizing the Gospel." *Encounter* 23 (1962): 190–95.

"Christ's Promise Fulfilled." *Digest of the Proceedings of the Consultation on Church Union* (1963) II: 135–59.

"Hunger for Catholicity." *Religion in Life* 32 (1963): 169–78. German translation: *Ökumensiche Rundschau* 12 (1963): 1–11.

"Behold, I Make All Things New." With Lukas Vischer. *Commission on Faith and Order* (Geneva), (1964): 5–32.

"The Development of Interconfessional Research." *Proceedings of the National Workshop on Christian Unity* (Baltimore), (1964): 24–34.

"Interconfessional Research." *Vital Speeches of the Day* 30 (1964): 343–46.

"Brahms and the German Requiem." *Theology Today* 22 (1965): 236–49.

"Church Renewal and Social Renewal." *Interpretation* 19 (1965): 3–15.

"A Note on *Luke* 22:37." *Novum Testamentum* 7 (1965): 128–34.

"Pictures of the Apostolic Church" (Consultation on Church Union). *Mid-Stream* 4 (1965): 247–72.

"The Apostolic Structure of the Church." *Andover Newton Quarterly* 6 (1966): 15–37.

"Ontology and Ecclesiology in the Apocalypse." *New Testament Studies* 12 (1966): 89–105.

"Ecumenism and the Seminary." *Theological Education* 3 (1967): 308–16.

"Karl Barth, Theologian." *New Republic* 160 (1969): 12–14.

"An Apocalyptic Adjective." *Novum Testamentum* 12 (1970): 218–22.

"The Idea of Incarnation in *1 John.*" *Interpretation* 24 (1970): 291–302.

"Paul's Teaching on the Eucharist in *1 Corinthians.*" *Worship* 44 (1970): 83–92.

"Some Glimpses of Luke's Sacramental Theology." *Worship* 44 (1970): 322–31.

"Communication and Community." *Theology Today* 27 (1970): 140–54.

"Yes or No: The Demand for Honesty in the Early Church." *Novum Testamentum* 13 (1971): 1–13.

"The Influence of Ecumenical Developments on New Testament Teaching." *Journal of Ecumenical Studies* 8 (1971): 286–99.

"Dear Theo: The Kerygmatic Intention of *The Book of Acts.*" *Interpretation* 27 (1973): 131–50.

"Heavens." *Reformed World* 32 (1973): 250–55.

"The Eschaton." *Spectrum* (Association of Adventist Forums, Loma Linda, Calif.) 5.1 (1973): 32–38.

"Matthew, Evangelist, and Johann, Composer." *Theology Today* 30 (1973): 243–55.

"Salvation in the Apocalypse." *Risk* (World Council of Churches) 9 (1973): 78–86.

"Jesus' Audiences According to Luke." *Novum Testamentum* 16 (1974): 81–109.

"A Note on *Luke* 17:7–10." *Journal of Biblical Literature* 93 (1974): 82–87.

"Ecumenical Theology—Profession or Vocation?" *Theology Today* 33 (1976): 66–73.

"We Don't Know Where—*John* 20:2." *Interpretation* 30 (1976): 125–39.

"The Beloved Disciple in the Fourth Gospel." *Novum Testamentum* 19 (1977): 105–23.

"The Audience of the Fourth Evangelist." *Interpretation* 31 (1977): 339–54.

"Four Bible Studies." Reformed World 34 (1977): 332–53.

"The Vocation of the Church: Some Exegetical Clues." *Missiology* 5 (1977): 13–37.

"Evangelists, Ecumenists, and *John* 17." *Theology Today* 35 (1978): 5–13.
"*John* 17:1–11." *Interpretation* 32 (1978): 175–80.
"Some Archetypal Origins of Apocalyptic Predictions." *Horizons in Biblical Theology* 1 (1979): 105–35.
"The Bible and the Congregation." *Theology Today* 38 (1981): 350–56.
"Living Stones." *Ecumenical Review* 34 (1982): 238–48.
"Christ and the Congregation: *1 Corinthians* 5, 6." *Review and Expositor* 80 (1983): 341–50.
"The Death of Death." *Drew Seminary Gateway* 54 (1983): 17–25.
"The Functions of *John* 21." Journal of Biblical Literature 102 (1983): 85–98.
"Holy People, Holy Land, Holy City." *Interpretation* 37 (1983): 18–31.
"*Matthew* 28:1–10." *Interpretation* 38 (1984): 59–63.
"Homiletical Resources: *John* 6." *Quarterly Review* 5 (1985): 68–90.
"J. S. Bach and Today's Theologians." *Theology Today* 42 (1985): 201–10.
"A Theology of the Heart." *Worship* 63 (1989): 246–54.
"The Holy and the Sacred." *Theology Today* 47 (1990): 5–12.
"Far as the Curse Is Found: The Point of Revelation 12:15–16." *Novum Testamentum* 33 (1991): 71–77.
"Writing on the Ground: The Puzzle in *John* 8:1–11." *Horizons in Biblical Theology* 13 (1991): 23–37.
"Blasphemy Backdated." *Horizons in Biblical Theology* 15 (1993): 38–51.
"The Promise of Life in the Gospel of John." *Theology Today* 49 (1993): 485–99.

Scripture Index

Old Testament

Genesis
1—2 1, 78–80, 84, 95, 108, 113, 118, 123
1:2 113
1:3 101, 117
1:21 31
1:25–26 31, 38
1:28 39
1:30 31
2:2 87, 92
2:7 76, 93
2:16–17 23, 25, 67, 90
3—4 xii, 1, 67–68, 95, 113
3 36, 48, 50, 55, 76, 78, 85, 114
3:1 32, 71, 90
3:3–5 23, 90
3:6–8 24–25, 108
3:14–15 17, 97
3:15 25, 32–34, 46–48, 51, 79, 105
3:16 26–27, 98
3:17–19 16–17, 38–39, 76, 93, 117, 122
3:20 25, 98
3:24 xv, 25
4:1–6 27, 90, 117
4:10–12 xi, 16–17

5 68, 78
5:5 23
6:13 115
7:17–23 117
8:11 115
11:1–9 50
46:32 12

Exodus
16:4–5 122
16:18–19 122
16:35 122

Deuteronomy
8:3, 16 123

Joshua
5:12 122

Nehemiah
9:20 122

2 Kings
19:21 28

Psalms
8 79–80
37 119
78:24 122
91 35

Isaiah
25:7 76
37:22 28

49:6 108
53:9–12 42–43, 117
61 36
66:7–9 27

Jeremiah
18:13 28
31:2–4 28
31:21 28
33:12–13 12

Lamentations
2:13 28

Ezekiel
34:1–3 12
34:12–20 18, 20
34:23–31 14–16

Hosea
4:2 96
13:14 76

Joel
2:18–32 50

Nahum
3:1 96

Habakkuk
2 96

Zechariah
9:9 20

Apocrypha

Sirach
22:24   96

2 Maccabees
14:18   96

2 Esdras
1:19   122
3:21–26   4–5
6:1–6   5, 82–84
6:30   4
6:39–40   92
7:11   4
7:42   92
7:45–64   4
7:70   5
9:5–6   6, 86

4 Maccabees
15:30   26
18:6–9   26

New Testament

Matthew
3:1–12   105–6
3:16   115
4:1–11   121
5:5   118–20
5:10–12   118, 123
5:43–48   120
6:9–13   13, 58, 120–23
9:6   121
10:1   121
10:7–8   114
10:16–25   114–15, 123
11:25–30   120
12:28   121
12:50   120
16:19   121
18:18   121
21:5   120
23:9   120
23:30–37   79, 105–7, 128
24:1   107
26:4   106
27:16, 25   107
28:18   125

Mark
1:7–15   34

6:39   39
8:31–35   109–10
11:9   20
14:51–52   25

Luke
1:2   8
1:8–20   11
1:26–38   8, 11, 21–27, 49, 52
1:42   25
1:51–53   24
1:77–79   8–9
2:7–20   16–36
2:34–35   8, 39
2:38   60
3:6   33
3:22   115
4   34–36
4:28–30   54
4:34   36
4:41   36
5:17–26   37
9:1   37, 48
9:21–24   39, 59
9:41–45   37, 40
10:3   10
10:17–19   34, 37, 48, 121
11:15, 20   37
11:42–52   18, 38–39, 43, 53, 55, 79
12:32   18
13:16   37
13:31–33   54
16:8   38
17:1   8
18:34   40
19:37–41   19–20
19:47–48   54
20:19, 26   54
22:2   54
22:20   18, 41–42, 110
22:24–27   43
22:29–30   43, 48
22:31–38   42–43, 110–11
22:40–46   40
23:13   44
23:18–25   44
23:34   40, 44
23:35–46   8, 36, 45

24   40
24:1   8
24:11   60
24:13–32   40–41
24:36   9
24:44–49   8, 41–42, 49, 54

John
1   xiii, 88
1:1   82
1:3–5   85, 92, 94, 101
1:10–13   84–85, 87–89, 92–96, 100, 116
1:14–15   83, 86, 97, 100
1:17–18   82–84, 97
1:27   83
1:30, 36   83
1:47–48   85
2:11   85
3   86–88
3:4   93
3:16   87
3:29   83
4:34   91
4:37   72
5   87
5:10–18   91–92
5:21–24   71
5:25–28   86, 89–90, 92
5:36–38   91–92
5:46   89
6:27–35   91–92, 122
6:50   122
8   89–90, 96
8:1–11   xii, xvi
8:39–47   92, 95
9   90–92, 100–101
9:5   101
9:33   101
10   13, 95–96
10:30   93
12:24–25   72
12:38   101
13:1   85, 96
14   101
14:8–11   93
14:23   93
14:27   102
15:10   102
15:16   xiv, 102

15:19 96
16:1–3 96, 102
16:21 98
17 100
17:1–5 84–86
17:10 96
17:11 93
17:21–22 93
20:17 86
20:21 86, 94
21:1–8 25, 38
21:15–23 102

The Book of Acts
1:2 48
1:4–5 49
1:11 49
2 49–53
3:14–26 52
4:5, 8 52
4:12 61
4:23–28 52
4:31–37 52–53
5 53
5:29 113
5:31–39 54
6:7–11 54–55
7:45–46 113
7:51–58 55
8:7–8 56
8:17–24 56
9:1–5 55, 128
9:16 56
10:34–48 56
13:33–37 66
13:39–41 108–9
13:46–47 108
19:16 25
20:24–30 19
22:3–5 54
22:14–15 56
24:1–13 113
26:17–18 40, 57

Romans
4:17 71
4:25 76
5—8 127
5:12 4, 68
5:18–21 xiv, 127
6:3–11 63

8:1 60
8:2 xv
8:10–11 71
8:20–21 xiv, 112
8:22 98
8:28–30 xiv, 127
8:38–39 xv, 112
9:3 128
11:32 129
11:36 128

1 Corinthians
1:2–9 63
1:18–25 80
1:26–29 73
2:7–8 24, 79
3:5–9 63, 70
3:21–23 77
6:15 77
7:37 98
8:6 78
9:11 70
12:12–13 75, 77
13 63
13:5 69
15 xiii, 63
15:1–2 63
15:3–11 64, 76
15:9 112
15:11 65
15:12–19 65–67
15:20–23 65–68, 71, 77
15:24–28 78–79
15:31 74
15:34 80
15:35 69
15:36–42 69, 71, 73, 77
15:43–44 73
15:45 71
15:48–49 74–75
15:51–53 76
15:54–57 76–77
15:52–59 80
15:58 63, 71, 76

2 Corinthians
3:2–6 71
3:18 72, 75
4:4 79
4:6 74
4:7–14 71–72

5:1–5 25
5:14–17 3, 74, 112
5:21 73
9:6 70
9:9–15 70
13:13 3

Galatians
1:3–5 4
1:13–16 55
2:19–20 111–12
3:15 35
3:28 112
4:4–7 32, 112
6:14–15 111

Philippians
2 24
3:6 64
3:20–21 73

1 Thessalonians
4 66
5:18 76

1 Timothy
5:11 98

Hebrews
1:2 xv, 127
1:10 92
2:5, 9 127
2:14–18 113, 127
4:1–11 127
4:3–4 92
4:13 25
4:15 113
6:4–8 112–13
10:32 113
12:4 113
12:18–24 113
12:24 12, 113, 127

1 Peter
1:2 118
1:18–19 117
1:20–21 117
2:9–10 116–17
2:22–24 117
3:18–20 117
3:22 117
4:8 118

1 John

1:7	100
1:8–10	99
2:1–2	99
2:12–16	100
2:16–17	99
2:29	99
3:2	116
3:7	115
3:9–10	99–100
3:11–12	115–16
3:14	116
3:15	115
3:16	100, 116
4:2	100
4:7	99
5:1	99

The Book of Revelation

2:7	45, 122
2:17	122
3:17–18	25
12:1–4	98
12:7–12	20, 121
12:9	34
12:13–17	xi, xvi
14:1–5	52
16:15	25
20	80
21:1	80
22:2	xv

Apostolic Fathers

Ignatius to the Ephesians

19:1	24

The Epistle of Barnabas

7:2	71

Hermas, Similitudes

9.16.1–7	71

The Epistle to Diognetus

5:11–17	71
12:7–8	26, 28

The Protoevangelium of James

13:1	26

This book is due for return on or before the last date shown below.